How to Get Over Your S**t

Reset your Nervous System to Reclaim
Your Power, Clarity and Confidence

CLAIRE WU

First published by Ultimate World Publishing 2025
Copyright © 2025 Claire Wu

ISBN

Paperback: 978–1–923425–43–9
Ebook: 978–1–923425–44–6

Claire Wu has asserted her rights under the Copyright, Designs and Patents Act 1988 to be identified as the author of this work. The information in this book is based on the author's experiences and opinions. The publisher specifically disclaims responsibility for any adverse consequences which may result from use of the information contained herein. Permission to use information has been sought by the author. Any breaches will be rectified in further editions of the book.

All rights reserved. No part of this publication may be reproduced, stored in or introduced into a retrieval system, or transmitted in any form, or by any means (electronic, mechanical, photocopying, recording or otherwise) without the prior written permission of the author. Any person who does any unauthorised act in relation to this publication may be liable to criminal prosecution and civil claims for damages. Enquiries should be made through the publisher.

Cover design: Ultimate World Publishing
Layout and typesetting: Ultimate World Publishing
Editor: Marinda Wilkinson

Ultimate World Publishing
Diamond Creek,
Victoria Australia 3089
www.writeabook.com.au

Acknowledgements

For all my Breathe Into Peace early adopters, my first influencers, social media followers, buyers, private clients, group clients, and my loyal customers and fans.

It was always much more than breathwork or coaching or being on stage …

I've come to realise that among all the success I have had in life, the most important has been to overcome my mental health struggles and challenges around trauma. This realisation has changed how I define success, both personally and professionally.

Thanks for picking up this book and making it a part of your life. I hope this story gives you light and hope.

Disclaimer:

Please note that all names in this book have been changed. Any similarities to real persons in your lives are purely coincidental.

The information provided in this book is for general informational purposes only and should not be considered as medical advice. Always consult with a qualified professional before making any decisions regarding your health, treatment or medical condition. The author and publisher are not responsible for any actions taken based on the content of this book.

Praise for How to Get Over Your Sh*t

*How to Get Over Your Sh*t* is not just a book, but a journey of dialogue with yourself. It reminds us that no matter how many challenges and pain we have experienced in the past, we have the power to overcome difficulties and create a new life. I hope every reader can find resonance in it and bravely embark on their own path of growth.

Wendy Wong
Professor and Doctor of Physiotherapy,
Physical Therapy and Assistive Technology

HOW TO GET OVER YOUR SH*T

This book is a profound and moving journey through stories that will touch your heart and soul. It invites you to confront your inner struggles with courage and grace, empowering you to rise above life's obstacles and guiding you toward a place of peace and self-compassion. A true companion for anyone yearning to take better care of themselves and embrace life's challenges with renewed strength.

Dr Ji-Yu Lin
Child and Adolescent Psychiatrist,
National Taiwan Hospital

As someone who has turned challenges into opportunities, I deeply resonate with Claire Wu's *How to Get Over Your Sh★t*. Her book is a powerful guide to transforming pain into growth by embracing, not erasing, the past. Claire's blend of personal experience and clinical expertise offers practical tools for healing and self-discovery. Her insights on the nervous system and shifting beliefs are both relatable and transformative. This is a must-read for anyone ready to own their story and step confidently into the life they deserve.

Christine Wan
Director of C3 Education Group

PRAISE FOR HOW TO GET OVER YOUR SH*T

How to Get Over Your Sh*t shows you how to take personal control of how you respond to other people 'taking the piss' by understanding yourself, finding purpose and meaning in your life, learning your real value and developing internal resilience. It's full of valuable lessons from Claire's own personal journey, supported and reinforced with relevant examples and stories from her work with her clients. Her practical approach of 'bottom up' (using breathing, movement and community activity) and 'top down' (using conversation, mindfulness and shared experiences) to reset and regulate the nervous system are easily applied. This book is ideal for anyone wanting practical tools to shut down the negative influences holding them back and move forward, building a more positive self. There is something for everyone here!

Mark Comberford
Doctor of Physiotherapy,
Director at Comera Movement Science

Claire's book is a profound guide for anyone navigating life's challenges while striving to live with purpose and authenticity. Her approach to aligning with your values, setting goals and overcoming myths about personal growth is both practical and empowering. I was deeply moved by her vulnerability in sharing her journey, from finding belonging amidst culture shock to addressing the hidden scars of domestic violence. Her lessons in compassion and resilience offer a powerful reminder that healing and thriving are possible. This book is a beacon of hope for anyone ready to embrace their magnificence and create a life of intention and joy.

Dr Vanessa
Radiologist and Director of
Women's and Breast Imaging

HOW TO GET OVER YOUR SH*T

This book is a powerful blend of raw honesty, practical tools and heartfelt wisdom. Claire Wu has poured her soul into *How to Get Over Your Sh*t*, and it shows. Her ability to take complex emotional struggles and break them down into actionable steps is incredible. With exercises that push you to reflect deeply and stories that make you feel less alone, this book is a must-read for anyone ready to let go of self-doubt and step into their best self. As someone who has seen Claire's journey up close, I'm beyond proud of her for creating this transformative guide.

Kaley Chu
Author, Keynote,
Motivational Speaker at 100 Speakers

Contents

Acknowledgements	iii
Praise for How to Get Over Your Sh★t	v
Prologue	1
Chapter 1: Believe in Your Magnificence	5
Chapter 2: Acceptance, Growth and Boundaries	21
Chapter 3: Restoring Self–Love	37
Chapter 4: Overcoming Abandonment	55
Chapter 5: Beyond Bullying and Harassment	67
Chapter 6: Finding Hope in the Darkness	79
Chapter 7: Loving Your Body	89
Chapter 8: Reclaim Your Power	103
Chapter 9: Breaking Free from Abuse	113
Chapter 10: Uncover Your Success	123
Chapter 11: Breaking Free from Toxic Environments	133
Chapter 12: Letting Go of the Past	149

Chapter 13: Flourishing in New Beginnings   161
Chapter 14: Awaken Your Purpose and Thrive   175
Chapter 15: You Are Not Broken,
    You Are Simply Human   187
Final Words   205
This is Only the Start of Your New Beginning 205
Keynote & Workshop Available   211
Speaker Bio   213

Prologue

It was in Taipei, in 2005, that things started to unravel. I stood on the top of the school building, and felt like I needed to take a leap – not a leap of faith, but a leap to *end everything*.

Despite living the high life, attending the best medical school, dating the smartest and most handsome man, going to the coolest parties and taking frequent holidays, I was miserable.

I was constantly battling depression and anxiety. The pressure of being at a prestigious school was taking its toll. I was a mess.

The self-sabotage and criticism rolled in so fast that I barely noticed it coming anymore. My dad and mum were both controlling, calling me daily to tell me in no uncertain terms what I should do.

My general anxiety disorder (GAD) was out of control. My emotions were in a constant state of flux. There were days when I felt fine and I was dancing on a high, but in the next moment I found myself cringing in anxiety.

The sheer rage I felt at myself for being like this, for not being able to see a way out, pushed me over the edge.

Our new apartment was in the mountains. It was sparkling and fresh, staffed with friendly, middle-aged ladies. They were cheerful all the time, which was surreal in itself.

Dad and I were having another argument on the phone, which students walking past were trying to ignore. I looked at the trail next to the hills, which the school renovated, along with the apartments and the hilltop running track, with views across the whole of Taipei City – the skyline, buildings, lights, trees, clouds, rivers and the sea.

I stormed to my room, passing my new bed made of cedar as I walked towards the bathroom. I caught sight of myself, noticing the dark circles under my eyes. My eyes were red and swollen. Tears ran down my cheeks, glistening in the light. My mouth turned downward, trembling or quivering with each sob or attempt to speak.

My entire face showed signs of distress, with furrowed brows and a wrinkled forehead. I was only 18. My face was contorted in pain and grief, embodying the physical manifestation of my emotional state.

I shut down my phone. I clenched my fists. I felt trapped, like an animal in a cage. All this hard work to get into medical school and I was so unhappy, so mad. I paced back and forth. I took small, quick steps and tried to settle my thoughts and

PROLOGUE

calm myself down. But it wasn't possible. I was crazy. I was stuck in my head. I was stuck in hell.

I went to the rooftop of the apartment and stepped to the edge. It was wide and grey, dull and boring. I felt my legs and feet get heavier and my body collapsed. I just wanted the pain to stop.

'Please get help. The divine is always here to help you.'

I couldn't tell if the voice came from inside or out. I started crying again. A heavy, loud cry, like my body was trying to let go of everything. I was so exhausted. And so sad.

I couldn't live like this anymore. I didn't want to die, but I felt like dying. I was beyond shame, blame and despair. After all the effort, all the work to get here, and after creating this astonishing 'perfect life' I wondered how I was so pathetic. I was so sad and wanted to end my life. But I knew I needed to get help and keep going. Just like the voice said.

All I felt in that moment was tremendous pain. I was dying inside. I hated myself. I hated medical school. I hated my family. I hated everything and everyone.

I was in the darkest, deepest well. But I did find a way out.

CHAPTER 1

Believe in Your Magnificence

My dad always said I was going to do something special, something big. After reading my natal chart, he believed I was going to be the multi-millionaire in the family, despite wanting his firstborn to be a son. For him, an event in Year 8 confirmed my potential for future success. For me, the story feels like the beginning of my interest in personal development and business.

Our school fair was coming up, and my schoolmates were fighting over what to sell. They all had an opinion on what was best, including games, cakes, gum, mini travel products and jewellery. I took a different approach. It was summer, and

I knew the weather would be hot, so I started by asking myself a simple question: what do you want to eat and drink on a hot day? To me, the answer was clear – pizza and soft drink!

On the day of the school fair there were lots of stands selling different products, but most weren't having much success. On our stand, the pizza and soft drinks were selling out like crazy. We didn't make our products, we bought them in bulk from local shops. We divided them up, putting the pizza on plates and drinks in cups with ice. Overall, we invested a few hundred dollars. Since it was a hot, sunny day, just after lunchtime, our food and drinks were running out. We sold individual slices of pizza for $8 and drinks for $5. It was overpriced, and many kids were complaining about it – but they were still buying.

I won't forget the look on people's faces when I gave them their pizza and drink. They looked like they were saved. I was initially a bit worried about the pricing, but once I started selling and talking to strangers about their day, the connection that I made with them convinced them to buy from me. It was a powerful feeling. Who would say no to a young girl selling delicious pizza and a cold fizzy drink on a hot day?

But for me, it was more than that. It gave me a lot of confidence and it filled me with the belief that I could get what I wanted in life. I am the main creator of my life, and I am the manifestation of my desires and dreams.

However, I was not allowed to work during my teenage years. Most of my time was spent studying. My parents have a high standard of working conditions, and they thought it would be too exhausting and tiring to work as a child. What's more,

BELIEVE IN YOUR MAGNIFICENCE

for some in Asian culture, allowing your children to work is seen as a sign you are poor.

We were a standard upper–middle–class family and my childhood was fun, easy and I felt safe, most of the time. My siblings and I always had what we wanted. We went to private music lessons, played sport, learnt ballet and street dancing, and attended painting and art classes. My parents loved spending money on our hobbies and learning.

We went on holidays three times a year, usually to the countryside or sometimes overseas.

Yet I always felt my friends had more. They wore designer clothes, bags and shoes, and I disliked how they had better cars and houses with big backyards. I was envious, but every time I mentioned it, Mum would sourly tell me to join their family. My dad was the opposite. He was always encouraging me to use this desire to fuel success in my life.

*'Believe in your greatness.
Because what you believe is what you become.'*
– Udai Yadla

> When we believe in our magnificence, we lean into our values, to who we are as a person. We know where we're currently at. We understand our current identity, our habits, our feelings. We understand our relationships, our surroundings, and we can acknowledge where we are now and where we want to be. When we see ourselves for all the great things we have, all the amazing things we have accomplished, we can start defining our vision, defining what it is that we want from our next chapter.

BELIEVE IN YOUR MAGNIFICENCE

One of my value is authenticity – that's why whether I'm at full-time work or in my business, I'm all about honest, genuine and consistent actions.

Dallas rediscovered herself after 50

Dallas and I first met at a friend's birthday party. She was warm, approachable and full of laughter, but beneath her vibrant exterior was a woman carrying pain from her past.

Recently divorced, Dallas had been through sh*t that left her questioning her worth and direction in life. Yet, there was a spark in her, a desire to rebuild her life and create something meaningful.

At the time, Dallas had enrolled in a beauty therapy course and dreamed of opening her own salon. She knew what she wanted to do, but staying committed to her path felt like an uphill battle. Every step forward seemed to come with a wave of self-doubt, criticism and fear, clouding her ability to see the path forward.

One evening, after she shared her struggles with me, I asked her two simple yet powerful questions:

What values do you feel aligned to? What truly matters to you?

Dallas paused, her eyes lighting up with curiosity. It was clear she hadn't thought about her journey through this lens in the past.

We decided to explore this further and started working together. I asked her to write down the values she felt connected to – the ones she believed could guide her toward becoming the person she aspired to be. Dallas hesitated at first, unsure of where to begin, so I encouraged her to reflect on what brought her joy, what she admired in others, and what she wanted her salon to represent in her community.

BELIEVE IN YOUR MAGNIFICENCE

A week later, Dallas returned with a list. At the top were words like creativity, authenticity, connection, independence and growth. As she shared her values, I saw a shift in her — she seemed more confident and comfortable in her own skin. Talking about these ideals brought out a sense of clarity and excitement. For the first time in a while, Dallas began to see herself not as someone broken by her past but as someone rebuilding herself with purpose.

From there, we worked on how Dallas could incorporate these values into her daily life. Creativity became her outlet as she experimented with new techniques in her beauty therapy classes. Authenticity guided her interactions with others — she stopped pretending everything was perfect and allowed herself to be vulnerable. She shared her struggles with her peers. Connection reminded her to nurture relationships with those who truly cared. Independence fuelled her determination to launch her salon, and growth became her focus whenever self-doubt, judgement and perfectionism crept into her mind.

Dallas also started a Peace Journal, a journal with prompts to guide her through her worries, triggers and negative thoughts. Every evening she wrote down her worries and separated them into solvable and unsolvable worries. She chose to focus only on the solvable ones and listed out the steps she needed to take to solve them. She also wrote down three things she was proud of achieving in her day. This could be as simple as learning a new skill in class or choosing to rest when she felt overwhelmed or stressed. Slowly but surely, Dallas began to be kinder and more compassionate towards herself.

After we worked together for 6 months, Dallas truly blossomed. She completed her studies, gained confidence and took steps toward opening her salon. While challenges still arose, she faced them with resilience and grace, grounded in the values she had identified as her compass.

Watching Dallas transform into her best self was tremendously rewarding. She went from doubting her self-worth to embracing her beauty, strength and potential. Dallas' journey reminds us all that when we align with our values and nurture ourselves, we can overcome the toughest obstacles and create a career and life that reflects our deepest desire.

> Many of my clients find that they're focused too heavily on one area of life. For example, Dallas, who was previously a stay-at-home mum, devoted much of her time to family and relationships. But as she shifted her focus to building a beauty therapy business, she found that she needed to invest more time in her work. Over time, this balance allowed her to reconnect with her purpose – bringing joy and beauty to others' lives.

Andrew revisited his purpose and values

Andrew had always been a hard worker. In his early 30s, he was climbing the corporate ladder, earning promotions and collecting titles that others would envy. Yet, despite his success on paper, he often felt a sense of hollowness inside. Something was missing – a sense of purpose and connection to what mattered. He described his life as a series of check boxes, ticking off milestones without ever stopping to ask himself, 'Is this what I want?'

BELIEVE IN YOUR MAGNIFICENCE

The turning point came when Andrew faced burnout. One day, after a particularly exhausting work week, he found himself sitting in his car, unable to drive home. His chest was tight, his head spinning with thoughts of deadlines and expectations. That moment made him realise he couldn't keep living this way. He needed to understand why he felt so lost and figure out what he truly valued in his career and life.

Andrew decided to seek guidance. When we first sat down to talk, he shared his fears of being stuck in a life that didn't feel like his own.

'I don't even know what I'm working toward anymore,' he admitted. 'I just know I can't keep going like this.'

I encouraged Andrew to start by identifying his values – the principles that made him feel alive and aligned with his authentic self. It wasn't an easy exercise for him. Years of chasing external success and validations had left little room for introspection and self-reflection. But with some prompts and questions, Andrew began to uncover pieces of his inner world.

Over time, a list began to form: integrity, growth, creativity, community and adventure. These values weren't just words on paper, they were windows into the life Andrew wanted to live. Integrity reminded him to stay true to himself, even when societal pressures pushed him in another direction. Growth reflected his desire to learn, evolve and challenge himself. Creativity spoke to a long-buried love for storytelling and photography. Community reminded him of his longing for meaningful connections. Adventure reflected his dream of exploring new places and experiences.

Next, we worked on weaving these values into his daily life. Andrew started small. He carved out time to take a photography class, reigniting his creative spark. He volunteered at a local community centre, rediscovering the joy of helping others. He took weekend trips to nearby towns, satisfying his thirst for adventure while staying grounded in his busy schedule. These small steps began to create a ripple effect.

Andrew also began redefining his relationship with work. Instead of blindly chasing promotions, he sought projects that aligned with his values. He started advocating for integrity and innovation within his team, which not only made him feel more fulfilled but also inspired his colleagues and managers.

One day, Andrew shared with me a profound realisation: 'For the first time in years, I feel like I'm living my life instead of someone else's expectations.'

His new-found clarity on his values allowed him to find new ways of living and thriving.

Andrew's journey wasn't about making drastic changes overnight, it was about rediscovering what truly mattered to him and aligning his life with those values. Today, he lives with a sense of purpose that fuels his work, relationships and passions.

> Burnout is caused by chronic stress and pressure, which can come from work or home. It can affect anyone, and can be caused by a number of factors. For Andrew, it was unrealistic expectations, a high-pressure work environment, overwork, a lack of balance, minimal support and his perfectionism. After he uncovered his values, and accepted support, Andrew was able to regain balance and live a fulfilling life.

What are your values?

Look at the values listed in the table that follows. Note down those that you want to align with, that are meaningful to you. Often, we inherit our values from our parents, peers or societal expectations, or we may choose values we think others want us to adopt. It takes time to reflect and dig deep to uncover the values that truly belong to us, not those imposed by others.

HOW TO GET OVER YOUR SH*T

Personal	Professional	Social	Spiritual	Wellbeing
Integrity	Excellence	Justice	Gratitude	Vitality
Honesty	Hard work	Equality	Hope	Wellness
Courage	Innovation	Fairness	Love	Self-care
Authenticity	Collaboration	Freedom	Mindfulness	Nutrition
Accountability	Leadership	Sustainability	Faith	Physical fitness
Self-respect	Creativity	Inclusivity	Serenity	Mental clarity
Self-discipline	Efficiency		Compassion	Resilience
Confidence	Growth		Purpose	
Openness	Responsibility		Balance	
Humility	Teamwork		Connectedness	
Empathy				
Compassion				
Respect				
Trust				
Loyalty				
Kindness				
Generosity				
Forgiveness				
Communication				
Cooperation				

BELIEVE IN YOUR MAGNIFICENCE

Take your time reflecting on the values you have noted down, perhaps a few days or even weeks. When you are ready, identify the five values that are truly meaningful and resonate with you authentically.

My 5 main values are:

1. _____
2. _____
3. _____
4. _____
5. _____

> *'The starting place for your greatness is desire.*
> *The desire to succeed, to serve others,*
> *to keep on going no matter what.'*
> *– Assegid Habtewold*

What are your goals?

Where do you want to be in life in the next 5 to 10 years? After getting over your sh*t, who do you want to become? What kind of life do you want to live? And who do you want to surround yourself with?

It's important to understand where we currently stand in different areas of our lives, including work, relationships, leisure, personal growth, health and wellbeing. Setting goals in these areas will help you create a more balanced life.

HOW TO GET OVER YOUR SH*T

Before setting goals, it's important to understand there are two types: **stretch goals and impossible goals.**

Stretch goals are slightly out of your comfort zone but still within reach, pushing you to grow. When working toward these goals, your nervous system might activate, causing feelings of anxiety or even a fight-or-flight response. This is entirely normal. What's important is learning to balance your time in the stretch zone and returning to a calm state. Prolonged stress can lead to burnout, so ensure you allow yourself moments of recovery. However, the 'stretch' is necessary for growth.

A stretch goal is achievable with some discomfort and effort. For Dallas, her initial stretch goal was inviting one client to her home for an eyebrow treatment. It felt intimidating, but she could manage it by regulating through her breath.

On the other hand, an impossible goal feels completely unattainable. Achieving it would require you to become a drastically different version of yourself. For Dallas, the impossible goal might look like opening a large salon, managing 20 clients a week. Impossible goals are not meant to be achieved immediately – they are a guide to your ultimate potential. Even if you fail repeatedly, each step towards an impossible goal helps you grow in ways you never anticipated.

When setting goals, always ensure they align with your authentic self, not the expectations of society, family or others. They should reflect what truly matters to you. Here are five tips to guide you:

- Make it personal: your goals must be true to your desires, not influenced by others' expectations.

- Embrace the process: growth during the pursuit of a goal is the real success. Achieving it is a bonus.

- Balance ambition: avoid setting vague goals or too many at once. Focus on a few meaningful ones.

- Challenge your fears: doubts and fears don't mean failure, they are indicators of growth.

- Learn from the past: reflect on what helped you achieve goals before, identify patterns or mistakes and adjust.

As you strive for your goals, you will need to overcome barriers, including fear of failure. Remind yourself that failure is part of the process. Failures are lessons to help you grow and you succeed simply by growing. You may also feel worried about a lack of proof in your ability. You don't need evidence that you can do it – faith in the journey is enough. Overthinking and procrastination can also hold you back. By taking small, actionable steps, you build confidence and minimise the risk of perfectionism or fear paralysing you.

Healing self-practices to uncover your magnificence

1. Write down one stretch goal and one impossible goal in each of these five life areas: career, health, relationships, personal growth and leisure.

2. Reflect on what success means for you in each of these goals.

3. Break down your stretch goals into smaller, actionable steps.

4. Journal your fears, doubts and limiting beliefs.

5. Consider what your higher self would say to guide you.

Remember, your goals are a tool for growth. They don't define your worth but help you discover your potential. Whether you achieve them or not, the journey itself transforms you. So, take a deep breath, set your sights high, and embrace the process of becoming the person who achieves the impossible.

CHAPTER 2

Acceptance, Growth and Boundaries

When I was 10, we moved to the USA during my father's visiting scholar position. He had been considering immigrating, but the idea was not full–blown. We weren't prepared for the change, but we let it sink in and went with the flow.

Living in the USA reshaped my world view. It pushed me out of my comfort zone, taught me resilience and expanded my ability to embrace change. The experience enriched my life in ways I couldn't have imagined. The friends I made, the lessons I learned, and the new perspectives I gained have stayed with me, shaping who I am today.

Moving abroad isn't just about adapting to a new environment – it's about growing into a new version of yourself. While I didn't want to leave Taiwan, I'm grateful for the journey. It taught me that stepping into discomfort is often the first step toward discovering a broader, more beautiful world.

When we arrived, it was immediately apparent that the way people did things in the USA was very different from South-East Asia. Things we were accustomed to, like sharing food, caring for each other and fostering a sense of community, were not widely adopted. To this day, I still look back and wonder if it was cultural differences, language differences or just a fundamental difference.

Adjusting to life in the USA wasn't easy. I struggled with the language, despite thinking my English was decent before arriving. Practising and improving became a daily task, often accompanied by frustration. I missed my friends and the sense of belonging I had in Taiwan. Starting over felt lonely and daunting, but I realised that clinging to the past would hold me back. Slowly, I built new friendships, embraced change and found joy in the differences.

I had a good life back in Taiwan, but now I had a life here. I just had to keep looking forward. I needed to stand up for myself, and ask for what I want. I found that the US actually encourages this and values each individual, their input and their differences. This was something I didn't often see in Asian culture, where it's more about the collective, the community and the group. I have since wondered if that's part of the reason why mental health is such a big issue in both Australia and the USA, because individualism is more of a priority than community and collectivism.

ACCEPTANCE, GROWTH AND BOUNDARIES

I had heard so much about the USA – a land of opportunity, diversity and freedom. It was a place celebrated in movies and music, with many stories of success. But it was also a land of challenges. While the bright lights of Hollywood and the idea of a free country sounded appealing, I was not excited about leaving the life I cherished in Taiwan. However, my parents insisted that this was an opportunity to explore the world together as a family. In preparation, I'd read a lot, mostly about celebrities and all the fancy and positive things. I also read the immigrant's stories, how they started by cleaning the toilets or serving in an Asian restaurant before they resumed the usual jobs they had in their home country.

Culture shock and personal growth

When we arrived in Michigan, I was surprised – it was better than I had imagined. The movie-like idealism I'd envisioned gave way to the beauty of real life. Michigan's maple trees, red brick buildings and vibrant multicultural community immediately captivated me. MSU's university town was alive with diversity, filled with people from all corners of the world. It didn't take long for me to appreciate the new environment. Neither my siblings nor I realised at the time how profoundly this experience would shape our futures. What we thought would be a temporary adventure turned into a life-changing journey: my sister eventually immigrated to the USA, and I found my path to Australia.

The cultural differences were striking and the diversity of people I met was eye-opening. Coming from Taiwan, I had my own biases and assumptions. Interacting with friends from places like China, Iran, Korea, Japan, South Africa and Finland broadened my world view. I discovered that preconceived notions are barriers to genuine understanding.

In this way, I learned that culture shock isn't necessarily a bad thing. It taught me to understand that the discomfort, confusion and frustrations are temporary. I learned about the culture by following it. When Halloween came, we all dressed up and went trick-or-treating. When Thanksgiving Day came, we learned to make roast turkey and vegetables. It was fun and made us feel like part of the country and the culture. My mum made a lot of Korean and Japanese friends and learned to make kimchi, sushi and other Korean foods. From time to time, she would still make food from Taiwan – beef noodles, dumplings, fried rice and chicken soup. It was beautiful because it connected us to home. We missed home.

While Michigan was multicultural and inclusive, our family occasionally faced discrimination, often rooted in ignorance rather than malice. For instance, at a restaurant, we were misjudged for ordering fewer meals than people at our table – the waitress had a really poor attitude. My father's decision to leave a generous tip changed the waitress's attitude, but I struggled with the idea of rewarding disrespect. This experience taught me to separate others' judgements from my self-worth. Discrimination, I realised, often stems from a lack of understanding or exposure. This perspective became a cornerstone of how I approach similar situations today.

> *'Whatever you are willing to put up with is exactly what you will get.'*
> *– Unknown*

ACCEPTANCE, GROWTH AND BOUNDARIES

Being overseas genuinely changes you. It shifted my belief system and my nervous system. It pushed me into my stretch zone, widening my window of tolerance. It helped me to handle more challenges and cultural differences in a positive way. I've learned to balance compassion and boundary-setting, understanding that ignorance is not my burden to bear. I encourage others to open dialogues, foster understanding, and when necessary, walk away from toxic environments.

Being in the USA allowed me to embrace diversity, equity and inclusion. This is me representing Japan in the Mocked United Nations Club.

Rose's experience in Perth, Australia

One of my clients, Rose, relocated to Perth a few years ago from India. Her partner works in the marine industry and she works in the coaching space. When we met, she explained how she would get upset and angry when asked questions that felt discriminative to her cultural background, skin colour or ethnicity. She was unsure how to deal with it, so I suggested six key areas she could focus on to change her perspective and response.

1. Be compassionate

Keep in mind that some people have had limited exposure to different cultures. They may have a set of ideas and assumptions about what another culture is like and it can be difficult for them to understand your ethnicity and cultural background, which can lead to discrimination and negative opinions. Be compassionate, kind and understanding. Behind discrimination, there are often struggles, fears, judgements and doubts.

2. Don't take it personally

This behaviour can come from ignorance and fear, often with roots in their upbringing. Understanding this can make it easier to take a compassionate approach. I asked Rose not to take it personally, because the actions of others reflect their belief system, nervous system and experiences. It's not related to you directly. Separate their reactions from you, so you can respond, rather than react. Respond with empathy instead of frustration. I am not saying that it's okay to discriminate. Being empathetic doesn't change the fact that they've made a mistake. When we can consider where they're coming from, their mental, physical and past struggles, it can help you understand them and the situation a little bit better.

ACCEPTANCE, GROWTH AND BOUNDARIES

3. Set boundaries

Being compassionate doesn't mean that we allow ourselves to be treated badly. I encouraged Rose to set boundaries, to be upfront about how she felt and how the behaviour affected her. When we set boundaries, we're able to protect ourselves and approach interactions with more understanding. We can communicate calmly, open the dialogue, and share with others how they are affecting us. I suggested she tried responses like:

'Unfortunately the way you speak about my culture makes me feel very uncomfortable. It feels like you're looking down upon me, like I am inferior to you.'

'You might not mean it, but your assumptions about what I do and why I am here in Australia are not true. It feels really hurtful.'

Responses like this gives them time to explain their viewpoint, so we can try to understand.

4. Move forward and seek support

We always want to continue moving forward. Ideally the other person will apologise for their behaviour. We hope to challenge their assumptions, to allow them to be open to change, so they can do better next time. We can also seek support when it feels hard to navigate, because the discrimination might bring up a lot of negative memories and past sh*t events that have happened to us. I suggested Rose reach out to her friends and family and share the experience, as they are likely to offer encouragement, support and kindness to help her process this experience.

5. Lead by example

We want other people to be compassionate, have respect, show kindness and integrity – and we want to demonstrate the same. When we avoid making assumptions about other people and their culture, background and ethnicities, and we take time to learn about their differences, we lead by example.

6. Reset your nervous system

When Rose was triggered, she was in a fight or flight state. She wanted to shout or slap the person in the face. I suggested she focus on breathing out slowly, practising long and consistent exhales. When we exhale, it stimulates the vagus nerve, slows down the heart rate and calms the body. It helps you return to a connected state.

> Moving to a new country is stressful. It challenges our nervous system to learn about our triggers, belief system and our bodily response to changes. Sometimes we face discriminations and conflicts that are uncomfortable. At times, we need to accept the challenge, so we can grow and learn. For Rose, the discrimination felt extremely uncomfortable, but after she understood her nervous system and reactions, she was able to regulate herself when she was triggered. She learned to set boundaries and stand up for herself.

Huang set boundaries in the face of racism

Huang had always been proud of her heritage. A talented marketing manager in her late 20s, she had moved to a new city to pursue her career and realise her dreams. Yet, in this new

ACCEPTANCE, GROWTH AND BOUNDARIES

environment, she began facing subtle and overt instances of racism. From offhanded 'jokes' at work to outright hostility in public spaces, these experiences left her feeling hurt, confused and unsure of how to respond.

The first time it happened at work, Huang was in a meeting with her team. A colleague made a stereotypical comment about her background, disguised as humour. The room laughed, but Huang felt her chest tighten and face flush. She said nothing at the time, unsure of how to react without making the situation worse. Later that day, she replayed the moment in her head, feeling both angry at the comment and frustrated with herself for staying silent.

Over time, these experiences began to pile up, affecting Huang's confidence and mental wellness. She realised that ignoring them wasn't working. She needed to address the behaviour and set boundaries to protect herself. But the question loomed: how?

Huang reached out to a me, as I had faced similar challenges in school and at work. I chatted with her about how racism, whether subtle or overt, was never acceptable and how staying silent could sometimes reinforce the behaviour. I encouraged her to prepare for these situations by developing clear and assertive ways to respond. 'Setting boundaries,' I explained, 'isn't just about confronting others. It's about honouring where you stand and teaching others to do the same.'

The next time a colleague made a racially insensitive remark, Huang took a deep breath and spoke up. 'I don't find that funny,' she said calmly. 'Comments like that are harmful and inappropriate.' The room went silent. Her colleague muttered an apology, clearly embarrassed, but Huang felt a surge of empowerment. 'Please don't do that again.' She had drawn a line and defended herself with pride and dignity.

Setting boundaries wasn't always easy. There were moments when Huang felt vulnerable or second-guessed her decisions. But with practice, she became more confident in articulating her feelings and addressing problematic behaviour. She learned to approach situations with both firmness and grace, saying things like, 'I'm uncomfortable with that comment' or 'That's not acceptable to me.' Her responses were clear, respectful and effective.

Outside of work, Huang also learned to navigate public encounters with racism. If someone made a nasty comment in public, she would calmly say, 'Please don't speak to me that way.' If the situation escalated, she would prioritise her safety and seek support from others nearby.

As Huang continued to set boundaries, she noticed a shift – not just in how others treated her, but in how she viewed herself. She began to feel more empowered, confident and proud of her ability to stand up for herself. Setting boundaries became a way of reclaiming her voice and asserting her value.

> What Huang did was a reminder that confronting racism and setting boundaries is an act of courage. By choosing to speak up, she not only protected herself but also contributed to a broader culture of respect and accountability. Through standing up for herself, Huang also showed strength for others facing similar challenges.

ACCEPTANCE, GROWTH AND BOUNDARIES

'Daring to set boundaries is about having the courage to love ourselves even when we risk disappointing others.'
— Brené Brown

Culture shock and the nervous system

Culture shock is a psychological and physiological response to experiencing an unfamiliar cultural environment. It often arises when individuals encounter new norms, values and practices that differ significantly from their own, triggering a sense of disorientation. This adjustment process can place considerable stress on the nervous system, which plays a central role in managing our responses to such challenges.

The autonomic nervous system (ANS), particularly its sympathetic branch, is activated during culture shock. This 'fight or flight' response can lead to heightened stress levels, anxiety and even physical symptoms such as a racing heart or digestive disturbances. The brain perceives the unfamiliar environment as a potential threat, leading to increased cortisol production, which can exacerbate feelings of overwhelm.

Simultaneously, the parasympathetic nervous system (PNS), responsible for calming the body, may struggle to restore balance. This imbalance can leave individuals feeling emotionally drained and physically fatigued. However, with time and conscious regulation of the nervous system, such as through mindfulness, breathwork or other body–based techniques customised to suit, individuals can gradually adapt to the new cultural environment. Understanding that culture shock is a natural part of transitioning allows people to be more compassionate with themselves as they reset their nervous system and adjust to a new sense of normalcy.

Understanding boundaries

Boundaries are limits you set to protect your physical, emotional and mental wellbeing. They define what you are comfortable with and how you allow others to treat you. Boundaries are essential for self-respect, healthy relationships and personal growth. Types of boundaries include:

- **Physical boundaries** relating to your personal space and physical needs.
  E.g. 'I need some alone time to recharge.'
- **Emotional boundaries** to protect your feelings and emotional energy.
  E.g. 'I'm not comfortable discussing this right now.'
- **Time boundaries** to ensure your time is respected.
  E.g. 'I can't meet today; let's reschedule.'
- **Mental boundaries** to respect your thoughts, values and beliefs.
  E.g. 'I understand you feel differently, but this is what I believe.'
- **Material boundaries** to protect your belongings and financial resources.
  E.g. 'I'm not able to lend you money right now.'

How to set boundaries

Step 1: Understand your needs
Reflect on what makes you feel safe, nourished, respected

ACCEPTANCE, GROWTH AND BOUNDARIES

and supported. Identify situations where you feel drained, overwhelmed, taken advantage of, resentful, fearful or upset.

Step 2: Communicate clearly
Use 'I' statements to express your needs without blaming others, for example, 'I feel overwhelmed when I'm interrupted. Can we discuss this after I finish my task?'

Step 3: Be firm but kind
Stick to your boundary even if it feels uncomfortable, for example, 'I understand you're upset, but I need to step away and process this.'

Step 4: Expect resistance
Some people may push back when you set boundaries, especially if they've benefited from your lack of them. Stay consistent.

Step 5: Practise self-awareness
Pay attention to how certain interactions affect you. If something feels off, or you felt resentment or regret, it's a signal to set or adjust a boundary.

Step 6: Start small
Begin by setting boundaries in low-stakes situations to build confidence. Say no to something you don't want to do each day and see what happens. Some examples include:
- In relationships: 'I'm happy to help you, but I need at least 24 hours' notice.'
- At work: 'I'm available to answer emails during work hours, but not after 6pm.'
- With family: 'I appreciate your advice, but I've already made my decision, thank you.'

Healing self-practices to foster personal growth

1. Start your day with meditations, breathing or other movement practices, as this can ground and centre yourself to set a positive tone for the day. It will help you cultivate awareness of your thoughts and feelings, reducing stress and anxiety in the morning.

2. Keep a daily journal or notebook to reflect on your experiences, emotions and thoughts. This practice can help you process complex feelings, track patterns in your behavior, and clarify your goals and aspirations. If you need some help getting started, you can access some pages from my Peace Journal here: https://breatheintopeace.com/products/journal-pages

3. Make it a habit to reflect on what you are grateful for each day. Write down three things you appreciate daily, or the lessons you have learned. It could be the 'no' you just said, or the realisation that you need to set firmer boundaries. This can shift your focus from what's missing, to what you have gained and learned each day.

4. Build a network of friends, family or colleagues who respect your boundaries and support your journey. This network can provide encouragement and reinforce your efforts to maintain these limits, making it easier to stay consistent.

ACCEPTANCE, GROWTH AND BOUNDARIES

5. Regularly reflect on the effectiveness of your boundaries and make adjustments as needed. This could be done through journalling or meditation. Assess whether your boundaries are being respected and if they still align with your personal growth goals. Adjustments might be necessary as your situation and relationships evolve.

CHAPTER 3

Restoring Self-Love

*The following content includes stories of abuse that may be triggering. Please make sure you take care of yourself and seek support before you read, or you may wish to skip this chapter.

When we experience trauma, it changes not only our brain, but also our body, including the nervous system, physiology, biology and neural pathways. Whether small or large, trauma has a significant impact on our lives because it changes us on so many levels.

After living in the US for a few years, my younger brother, sister and I wanted to immigrate. We had so much fun and enjoyed being with people from all over the world. The big lake in Michigan was just like a wide ocean with the breeze, light and reflections from the water, and the beautiful cold weather with white snowflakes amazed me. We often skied in winter, and in the summer, we spent our time on the water, kayaking and stand-up paddle boarding.

But in the end, my parents chose not to move to the US. They felt like the immigration process was too long. They also didn't want to start from scratch, doing labour jobs like cleaning, waitressing and removal work. My parents were typical PhD academics. For them, their genius lay in their brain and teaching, not in physical work. We returned to Taiwan when I was 15 years old. My parents wanted to make sure that I transitioned back to the school system in South-East Asia smoothly, so I would not lag behind. Little did I know, it was then that the real nightmare began …

My parent's attitude changed after we left the USA. I was limited to the friends I could have. In Taiwan, from junior high school onwards, classes were separate into three groups, depending on grades. I was only permitted to see friends that were at my level. If Mum saw me speaking with guys in a lower class, she would pull me aside and forbid me to spend time with them.

I had after-school private lessons and every night I was studying till 9 or 10pm. My life was books, knowledge and studies – nothing else. I was limited in the activities I could do. My dad drove me everywhere in his car and I was monitored almost 24/7. Once when I went to 7-11 just to get a snack, Dad came out of nowhere and shouted at me, 'You shouldn't be spending extra money on a snack!' He was monitoring me from the minute I left his car.

I was immediately immersed into this way of living – nonstop studying, lectures and school. I understood where the pressure was coming from. My mum taught Chinese at the prestigious school which I attended and my dad is a distinguished professor. The pressure to perform and do well consumed my parents.

Feeling not good enough

When I finished junior high in Taiwan, we had to take an entrance exam to determine which high schools we could attend. My grades were always excellent, consistently ranking in the top three. Naturally, my parents believed I'd get into the best high school. But I didn't.

I was accepted into the second-best school. My parents were devastated. My mother cried, overwhelmed with disappointment. She neglected me entirely, refusing to speak with me for months. As a teacher, she constantly compared me to her students, repeatedly telling me I wasn't good enough. I began internalising her language. My brain couldn't distinguish what was right and what was wrong. It absorbed whatever was coming from my environment. Eventually my mother's beliefs became my beliefs: I am not good enough.

In Year 6 I was mischievous, and one day, I made a girl cry. My mum was really upset – she felt ashamed and guilty. She got triggered and stressed, and said something like, *'I can't believe you'd do this. I just don't love you anymore.'* This experience left a heavy scar on me. The adult me knew my mum was trying to say she was disappointed in my behaviour and wished I wouldn't do it again. But it came out in a way that felt like punishment, like she was withdrawing her love as a consequence. Her words cut deeply. They created this belief in me that I wasn't loved and I wasn't lovable. I think that's the underlying reason I've worked so hard all my life, pushing myself relentlessly. There's nothing inherently wrong with hard work, but when it leads to burnout, breakdowns, exhaustion and fatigue, it becomes a problem.

Beating children is a common punishment in Asian culture, and I was beaten with belts, clothes hangers or fists. I can not remember how many times. I yelled and shouted but I couldn't run away. Afterwards, I'd kneel on the ground, crying, screaming, feeling like I didn't want to carry on living. I wanted to kill my family and bury them in their own blood. The desire for revenge burned as fiercely as the pain. At 18, I left home and never went back. I went as far as I could, travelling the world and I seldom return to Taiwan. Revenge wasn't forgotten, but it faded into the background. I had so much ahead of me – new places to explore, new people to meet and joys to embrace. Building a new life overseas wasn't easy. The challenges were constant, but it was my way of rewiring my nervous system and belief system and creating new neural connections to see the world differently.

> *'There are a lot of people who give you the message that maybe you are not good enough, and the best thing you can do for yourself is to block out all of that noise.'*
> *– Rachel Platten*

RESTORING SELF-LOVE

For those of us who've experienced physical abuse, sitting still or slowing down can feel terrifying. Your nervous system becomes wired to associate hesitation with danger. For years, I operated under the belief that slowing down was unsafe. But healing can start small. Begin by sitting in stillness for 3–5 minutes a day. Journal, breathe or do nothing. Over time, this teaches your brain that slowing down is safe.

The best revenge in life is success. This is me with my physiotherapy friends at school. We were stretching our ulnar nerve. I love anatomy, physiology, neuroscience and movement.

Shay left sh*t behind

One of my clients, Shay, endured domestic violence, toxic relationships and unhealthy workplaces. She had dreams of starting her own business but couldn't take action because she felt unworthy and incapable. Her painful memories held her back.

I encouraged her to list 10, 20, even 50 to 100 things she was good at, and the challenges she has overcome. This exercise rewired her brain to seek evidence of her strengths. But the mind alone isn't enough. We also worked on her body – improving her posture, including mobilising her thoracic spine, shoulders and head position. Her body held a lot of tension and pain, because she was constantly escaping from it. She dissociated and was often in a shut down, frozen state. When the body opens up, through the myofascial release, either actively or passively, it sends a message to the brain: *You are safe. You are in this body. It is safe to be in this body.*

> By practising these exercises daily and through our weekly meetings, Shay began to shift the perception she had of herself. Eventually, she had the courage to start her subscription box business and became highly successful, rooted in the belief that she was worthy of her awesome dreams.

Lee stopped self-sabotaging

Lee grew up in a household where love was conditional and approval was hard-earned. His family had high expectations and little tolerance for mistakes, often using shame and criticism as tools to enforce discipline. As a child, Lee internalised these patterns, learning to equate his worth with achievement and fearing failure as a sign of inadequacy. The emotional abuse he experienced shaped his adult relationships and decisions, leaving him stuck in a cycle of self-sabotage and self-hatred.

In his late 30s, Lee began to notice the patterns. Whenever things were going well – whether in his career, friendships or romantic relationships, he would find a way to derail them. He'd miss deadlines at work, withdraw from loved ones, or pick fights over minor issues. These behaviours left him feeling guilty and ashamed, feeding the narrative he had carried from childhood: 'I'm not good enough.'

When Lee and I met, he had a lot of migraines and suffered neck pain for many years. We worked on his body, relieving pain. He admitted he didn't understand why he kept sabotaging his own happiness. 'It's like I don't believe I deserve good things,' he told me during our first session.

Together, we explored the roots of his behaviours. It became clear that the emotional abuse he endured had created deep-seated beliefs about his worthiness and a fear of vulnerability. Lee had learned to expect rejection and pain, even in safe and supportive environments, and unconsciously recreated those dynamics to maintain a sense of control.

The first step in Lee's healing was awareness. I encouraged him to observe his thoughts and behaviours without judgement. When he felt the urge to self-sabotage, we worked on identifying the triggers. Was he afraid of failure? Did success make him feel unworthy? Was he trying to avoid potential rejection by ending things earlier? These reflections helped Lee see how his past was influencing his present.

Lee learned the power of self-compassion. When he caught himself slipping into self-sabotaging behaviours, instead of berating himself, he chose kindness. 'I'm doing my best,' he would remind himself. 'It's okay to stumble.'

Next, we focused on challenging the negative beliefs he had learned from his family. Lee began practising affirmations like, 'I am worthy of love and success' and 'My mistakes do not define me.' At first, these statements felt foreign, but over time, they started to chip away at the critical voice in his head. Lee also wrote letters to his younger self, offering the compassion and reassurance he had never received as a child.

A crucial part of Lee's journey was learning to set boundaries. Growing up, he had been taught to suppress his needs to please others. Now, he practised asserting himself in healthy ways. Whether it was saying 'no' to unreasonable requests or expressing his feelings openly, each small act of self-advocacy helped Lee rebuild his sense of worth.

RESTORING SELF-LOVE

> Over time, Lee saw a transformation. He began pursuing opportunities, nurturing his relationships without fear, and celebrating his achievements without guilt. While the scars of his past didn't disappear entirely, Lee no longer let them affect him or hold him back. He reclaimed his life, proving to himself that he was capable of growth, love and resilience.

'You have been criticising yourself for years, and it hasn't worked. Try approving of yourself and see what happens.'
– Louise Hay

Self-love through spirituality

Loving yourself sounds simple, but it's challenging for those of us who come from families where our needs and feelings were neglected. When you don't get validation as a child, or your needs aren't met, it becomes difficult to meet those needs for yourself as an adult. If a parent or caretaker constantly talks down to you, those words become imprints in your brain. A child doesn't distinguish between what's true and what's not, so you internalise it. It becomes your reality – that you won't be loved.

Later in life, setbacks and disappointments can reinforce that belief: *I'm not loved. I'm not cherished.* It takes a lot of time to overcome those beliefs. While challenging your thoughts is a good start, it's not always sustainable because your subconscious often takes over.

Yes, you can challenge your thoughts by writing down reasons why you're loved, listing the people in your life who care about you, and highlighting all the good things about yourself. These are helpful exercises. But the quickest way I've found to shift these deep-rooted beliefs is through spiritual practice.

Spiritual practices are powerful because they address beliefs at their core. They tap into the understanding that we are divine, that greatness is already within us. I began my own spiritual journey 10 years ago. I started embracing the idea that *I am great, I am genius and I am divine.*

A belief is just a thought you reinforce repeatedly. When you start with the belief that you're divine and worthy, it generates thoughts like, *I am amazing.* These thoughts, repeated often enough, become your truth.

In my spiritual practice, I often encourage clients to connect with nature, like walking through a forest, while repeating affirmations. For example, if the belief is 'I am loved', then the thoughts might flow like this: *I am great at cooking. I am great at being me. I am great at being funny. I am great at writing. I am great at creating graphics. I am great at moving forward.*

The thoughts naturally build on each other, and that's the power of spiritual practice – it reinforces beliefs that reshape your self-concept. Eventually, they become a part of you. For me, in 2019, I woke up one day and thought, *I am so great, I am so awesome,* and I've never looked back. That belief is now deeply embedded in who I am.

Shift your belief system

Pause now and write down 10 things you love about yourself. It could be anything, small or big. Read these on a daily basis — our repeated thoughts become our beliefs.

1. _____
2. _____
3. _____
4. _____
5. _____
6. _____
7. _____
8. _____
9. _____
10. _____

Shift your nervous system

We can use spinal movement to bring in more extension into the spine, sending a signal to the brain that we are confident, secure and safe in our body. The more we listen and be with our body, the more we can associate ourselves within.

Here's one thoracic movement that can improve the posture. Place both hands behind your head, elbows wide open. Breathe in, and breathe out as you close your elbows, flex your spine, and gaze down toward your belly. Breathe in, open up the chest, open up the elbows and look towards the sky. Repeat this 10 times and gradually, you will find there's more and more range in your spine.

When we feel inadequate, we shrink. We hunch our shoulders, hide our true selves and suppress our voices. We're afraid to share our thoughts or opinions because we don't believe they matter. Our posture provides a clue of our internal state – our internal state reflects on our posture.

It took several years to rewire my belief system and nervous system around 'not feeling good enough'. I discovered the power of spinal movement in my international Pilates training. Through body–based exercises, I changed my posture, breathing patterns, opened my shoulders, and adjusted my hips. These simple, daily movements have rebuilt my confidence and self–esteem, sending signals back to my brain and body, affirming that *I am worthy, I am enough, I am safe in my body.*

Another powerful technique is focusing on your exhale during breathing exercises. Lengthening your exhale activates the parasympathetic nervous system, calming your heart rate and signalling to your body that it's okay to relax. Start with 10 seconds and gradually extend it to 20–30 seconds or even 1 minute.

You can also rewire triggers by pausing before reacting. For example, if someone asks me for something, my instinct is to respond immediately out of fear. But now, I pause, prioritise, and address it when it fits into my day. By combining conscious breathing, movement and prioritisation, we can shift our nervous system state and regain control of our emotions.

Healing self-practices to restore self-love

An effective way to look after and love yourself is to plan pleasurable activities, things you enjoy doing that make you happy and content. Make a list of things that bring you happiness and aim to do at least one every day. Small, consistent acts of self–care remind you that you are deserving of love and joy.

To help you get started, take a look at the lists from my *Peace Journal*. Doing things you love creates good feelings, and when you feel good, subconsciously, it makes you feel like you're great, that you're loved, that you're amazing.

ACTIVITY FOR YOU

(CHOOSE 1 TO DO EACH DAY)

The following is a list of activities that might be pleasurable for you. Feel free to add your own pleasurable activities to the list.

- A day with nothing to do
- Soaking in the bathtub
- Singing around the house
- Lying in the sun
- Sleeping
- Driving
- Entertaining others
- Laughing
- Singing
- Flirting
- Sex
- Eating gooey, fattening foods
- Saving money
- Getting out of debt/paying debts
- Working
- Wearing sexy clothes
- Wearing comfy clothes
- Dressing up and looking nice
- Reflecting on how I've improved
- Travelling abroad/interstate/within state
- Meeting new people
- Discussing books
- Writing articles
- Cooking, baking
- Listening to music
- Acting
- Sightseeing
- Gardening
- Watching movies
- Taking care of my plants
- Playing with my pets
- Making lists of tasks
- Collecting things (coins, shells, etc.)
- Recycling old items
- Surfing the internet
- Debating
- Playing computer games
- Making jigsaw puzzles

RESTORING SELF-LOVE

ACTIVITY FOR YOU
(CHOOSE 1 TO DO EACH DAY)

The following is a list of activities that might be pleasurable for you. Feel free to add your own pleasurable activities to the list.

- Lighting candles
- Listening to the radio
- Getting/giving a massage
- Rearranging the furniture in the house
- Flying kites
- Erotica (sex books, movies etc.)
- Completing a task
- Listening to others
- Chatting on the internet
- Photography
- Being alone
- Writing diary/journal entries or letters
- Cleaning
- Reading
- Dancing
- Meditating
- Doing something spontaneously
- Going to a movie
- Going for a holiday
- Doing something new
- Doing woodworking
- Doing embroidery, cross stitching
- Doing arts and crafts
- Doing crossword puzzles
- Having quiet evenings
- Having discussions with friends
- Having family get-togethers
- Having class reunions
- Having lunch with a friend
- Having a political discussion
- Having coffee at a cafe
- Having a spa, or sauna
- Having a barbecue
- Going on a date

HOW TO GET OVER YOUR SH*T

ACTIVITY FOR YOU
(CHOOSE 1 TO DO EACH DAY)

The following is a list of activities that might be pleasurable for you. Feel free to add your own pleasurable activities to the list.

- Going to the gym
- Going for a run
- Going swimming
- Going to a party
- Going camping
- Going for a walk
- Planning my career
- Planning a day's activities
- Planning a career change
- Planning parties
- Planning to go for further studies
- Thinking I have done a full day's work
- Thinking about my past trips
- Thinking I'm an OK/great person
- Thinking about getting married
- Thinking about buying things
- Thinking how it will be when I finish school
- Thinking about my achievements
- Thinking I did that pretty well
- Thinking religious thoughts
- Thinking about my good qualities
- Thinking about retirement
- Thinking about having a family
- Thinking I'm a person who can cope
- Thinking about pleasant events
- Recalling past parties
- Remembering beautiful scenery
- Remembering the words/deeds of people
- Spending an evening with good friends
- Daydreaming

RESTORING SELF-LOVE

Which 5 activities will you do this week?

1. _____
2. _____
3. _____
4. _____
5. _____

CHAPTER 4

Overcoming Abandonment

One day, I woke up in the morning and no-one was at home. I searched all over the house, only to find that the car was gone. It wasn't until the evening that my parents and younger brother and sister returned. 'We thought you were sleeping and did not want to wake you,' was their explanation for not taking me with them. From that moment, a feeling of abandonment became my recurring nightmare. The dream kept evolving, becoming more and more painful.

In one of the dreams, I caught up with them at the garage before they left, and they had a car full of stuff. 'Claire, we cannot fit you in because it's full now,' my mother explained.

'Well, maybe you can chop me into pieces so I can fit in the car?' I suggested, trying hard to fit in. So they cut me into pieces and put bits and pieces inside the car.

I woke up in a sweat, heart beating fast and gasped. I started crying. My blood went cold and I could feel I was bleeding, not from the cuts, but in my heart. It was painful growing up, feeling like you were meant to be elite and a superstar, but at the same time, feeling abandoned and left behind. When I asked my parents about the story, they replied, 'We would never leave you behind alone in the house. You would be underage and it's illegal to do so.'

The story I had in my head could have been a projection. I'd always been the top in the school, and when I didn't get into the best high school, my parents ignored me. They stopped telling me that they loved me. All the love that I used to experience was replaced with harsh comments and nasty remarks.

It might have been something my inner child, the young Claire, created to make sense of what happened. She was meant to get into the best high school, but she didn't. She was meant to be loved through high school and university, but she was not. And then her mum and dad, verbally and physically, told her how disappointing it was. They disconnected, neglected her, gave her inconsistent care. And maybe that's how that nightmare began, and recurred over and over again.

A lot of us feel this way. It's like, when we don't achieve something, or get something, we feel like we're left behind. We feel abandoned. We are left out. We feel like we're no longer being looked after. And I think that fear is where it starts.

OVERCOMING ABANDONMENT

It's important to uncover how it all started … the root of the whole story. However, it's not necessary to keep revisiting the story again and again. Sometimes, though, it's hard not to, it just replays in your mind. I want you to acknowledge those feelings. Be honest with your thoughts, your emotions and your fears. You can write down what happened to you: how you felt left behind, how you didn't fit in, how you felt orphaned or how people seemed disappointed in you.

Remember that our memory as a child, and as a teenager, can be impacted by the amount of stress or cortisone level our nervous system can take. It's not solid. It can change shape. It can shift, and it can get twisted over time. So after my parents assured me this didn't happen, I knew I needed to go into something deeper, go into the subconscious and 'zap out' that memory.

I realised I needed 'spiritual surgery' to remove this story and rewire my nervous system and belief system. I went into a deep meditation in drumming. There, I spoke to my inner child and let her know I will never abandon her, I will always love her. She cried sitting next to me and told me how amazing and how beautiful I am.

I repeated this form of 'surgery' a few more times and the nightmares and dreams started to fade away. I stopped suffering and struggling with abandonment. It was 'zapped out' of my nervous system and belief system. For this to remain effective however, I had to create a reality that matched this 'new belief' and my 'new neuropathways'.

> *'Abandonment is the first step*
> *toward finding your true self.'*
> *— Unknown*

> I focus a lot on co-regulation, finding the right community and tribe that accept me, embrace me and see me for who I am. I am connected to multiple groups involved in hiking, camping, rock climbing, beach volleyball, speaking and writing. It keeps me active and engaged with others and the interactions help remind my inner self that I was not abandoned.

Josh overcame the fear of abandonment

Josh, a successful entrepreneur in his early 40s, had spent most of his life grappling with a deep fear of abandonment. As a child, his parents were emotionally unavailable, often prioritising their careers over spending time with him. Despite providing for his physical needs, they rarely offered the affection or attention Josh craved. This left him with an enduring belief that he wasn't worthy of love, a feeling that persisted into adulthood.

In relationships, Josh's fear of abandonment played out in painful ways. He either clung too tightly to his partners, or pushed them away, distancing himself emotionally to avoid getting hurt. Both patterns left him feeling lonely and unfulfilled. It wasn't until a long-term partner ended their relationship, telling him that his inability to trust or listen was the problem, that Josh decided to seek help.

OVERCOMING ABANDONMENT

When Josh and I began working together, I introduced him to a combination of body–up and brain–down techniques to address his fears. The body–up approach focused on calming and rewiring his nervous system, while the top–down approach targeted his thoughts and beliefs.

Body-up techniques

Josh's nervous system was often in a state of hypervigilance, a common response to early emotional neglect. We began with grounding practices to help him feel safer in his body. I taught him simple techniques, where he would focus on slow, deep, long breaths to signal to his brain that he was not in danger. He also practised spinal movement, releasing tension from his body to reduce feelings of anxiety and overwhelm.

We helped Josh reset his nervous system to re–enforce his feeling of safety and connection to his body. This helped him stay in his body and build a sense of calm and peace. We also incorporated gentle movement and stretching to release stored tension from his muscles and fascia.

Brain-down techniques

Once Josh felt more grounded, we worked on reshaping his thought patterns. He identified the core belief that had been driving his fear of abandonment: 'I'm not lovable unless I'm perfect.' We explored the origins of this belief and how it influenced his behaviours.

Josh began practising self–compassion, without judgement. He was kind and loving to himself, and he focused on self–care. We also introduced 'reframing', encouraging him to challenge negative thoughts when they arose. For example, when he felt a partner pulling away, instead of assuming, 'They're going to leave me' he learned to reframe it as, 'They might just need some space or alone time, and that's okay.'

As Josh continued practising these techniques, he began to feel more secure in himself and his relationships. He no longer let his fear of abandonment dictate his actions. Instead, he built a stronger sense of self-worth, allowing him to approach connections with trust and confidence. For the first time in years, Josh felt free from the shadows of his past and ready to embrace the future with an open heart.

> The combination of bottom-up and top-down techniques helped Josh bridge the gap between his mind and body. He reset his nervous system during moments of high anxiety and reframed his thoughts to avoid spiralling into fear-based reactions or anger outbursts. Over time, this approach created a positive feedback loop. Safer thoughts supported a safer body and calmer thoughts supported a calmer body, and vice versa.

Jessica healed her trust

Jessica, a 35-year-old marketing professional, had always struggled with feelings of abandonment. Her fear was rooted in a past relationship where her partner left unexpectedly, leaving her questioning her worth. When she entered a new relationship with her current partner, Mark, these fears resurfaced. Although Mark was supportive and loving, Jessica often felt anxious and insecure, convinced that he would eventually leave.

OVERCOMING ABANDONMENT

This fear manifested in Jessica's behaviour – frequent calls and texts to check in, overanalysing his tone or actions and withdrawing emotionally when she felt unsure. The pattern left her feeling drained and, ironically, distanced her from the connection she craved. Jessica knew she needed to break free from this cycle, so she sought help to address the root of her fears.

Her nervous system was often stuck in a state of hyperarousal, triggering fight–or–flight responses whenever she felt uncertain about her relationship. In our sessions, I introduced Jessica to a combination of bottom–up and top–down techniques aimed at resetting her nervous system and transforming her beliefs about relationships.

Once she began to feel safer and calmer physically, we worked on reshaping her thought patterns and addressing the core beliefs driving her fear of abandonment. Jessica recognised the belief that had been haunting her: 'If I'm not perfect, I will be abandoned.' We traced this belief back to her past experiences and acknowledged how it no longer served her. Jessica practised challenging her negative thoughts. For example, when Mark didn't respond to a text immediately, she replaced the thought 'He's losing interest' with 'He's probably busy, and that's okay.'

Jessica started journalling daily, noting moments where she showed herself kindness. She also celebrated her efforts to grow, reinforcing her sense of self–worth.

Combining customised techniques created a profound shift for Jessica. When she felt triggered, she reset her nervous system to calm her body. This immediately calmed her mind, Then, she reframed her thoughts, reminding herself of her inherent worth and the stability in her relationship. Over time, Jessica noticed her reactions becoming less intense, and her trust in herself and Mark grew.

> By resetting her nervous system and transforming her beliefs, Jessica freed herself from the grip of her fear. She learned that she was not defined by her past and could create a healthier, more secure connection in the present. Jessica now approaches her relationship with confidence and openness, knowing that she is enough, just as she is.

'Abandonment is never personal; it's a reflection of the person who walked away, not the one who was left behind.'
– Unknown

Exploring abandonment

Feeling abandoned often stems from deep emotional needs and attachments. As humans, we are wired for connection, and our sense of safety and belonging is deeply tied to the presence of reliable and supportive relationships.

Here are some common reasons why we may feel abandoned:

- **Early experiences:** If we experienced neglect, loss or inconsistent care as children, our brains may have wired themselves to fear abandonment as a survival mechanism. These early patterns can influence how we view relationships in adulthood.

- **Attachment styles:** People with insecure attachment styles (e.g. anxious or avoidant) may feel abandonment more acutely. This can stem from caregivers who were emotionally unavailable or inconsistent.

- **Loss or rejection:** Experiencing the loss of a loved one, a breakup or rejection from someone we care about can trigger a deep sense of abandonment. It can feel like our emotional needs are no longer being met.

- **Self-worth issues:** If we tie our worth to others' approval or presence, when they are not there it can feel like a personal failure or a sign that we're unworthy of love.

- **Past trauma:** Unresolved trauma, especially from abandonment, can resurface in current relationships, making us more sensitive to perceived or actual distance from others.

- **Social isolation:** Feeling disconnected from a community or lacking close relationships can amplify feelings of being left out or unimportant.

Understanding the root of abandonment feelings can be the first step to healing. It's often helpful to explore these emotions with compassion and, if needed, seek support from a professional or trusted individuals. Recognising that these feelings are valid but not necessarily reflective of your true worth can lead to healthier relationships and greater mental resilience.

Self-care and self-love is critical in overcoming feelings of abandonment – getting enough sleep, eating nutritious meals, exercising and doing pleasurable activities. And most importantly, finding a group or community that supports you. Because when people support and care about you, something amazing happens – co-regulation. This is so important in healing and recovery.

Co-regulation happens when we're with other people, and their nervous system influences and calms ours. When we co-regulate, we help each other manage distressing emotions. It helps us feel calmer and more present in the moment. When we surround ourselves with people who are calm, loving, peaceful or happy, their energy rubs off on us. This happens because of our mirror neurons and the way our brains are wired for evolution and transformation.

That's why social interaction is so important. Other people can help us regulate ourselves. Other people's nervous systems have an effect on us. Co-regulation gives us a new perspective, one that is timely and transformative. It shows us that our problems are not just individual challenges to overcome, but shared experiences. We can relate to each other, and in doing so, we build resilience together.

Co-regulation is especially important in close relationships, such as between parents and children, partners or friends. It might involve verbal communication, physical touch or even non-verbal cues like facial expressions and tone of voice. For example, a calm and empathetic response from one person can help another feel safe and soothed during moments of stress or emotional dysregulation.

We're not just individually trying to heal or recover. We start to see that some of the things that happen to us are part of a collective trauma or collective suffering. And because we share these emotional experiences and interpersonal connections, we can help calm and regulate each other's nervous systems. Together, we can recover.

In coaching settings, co-regulation is a foundational tool. As a coach, I provide a stable and attuned presence, helping my clients navigate difficult emotions and develop better self-regulation skills over time.

Healing self-practices to overcome abandonment

Why do I feel abandoned?

_____
_____
_____

How do I attend to my need to be loved and cared for?

_____
_____
_____

Are there groups or communities (virtual or in-person) I could join to interact with others positively?

_____
_____
_____

CHAPTER 5

Beyond Bullying and Harassment

In Year 4 I was bullied badly. It started with one girl telling other people not to talk to me at school. It then became two, three and suddenly the whole of the fourth grade were not talking to me. It was so silent and quiet at school. Every time I walked into the classroom, people stopped talking and they refused to talk to me.

Luckily, there was one girl who refused to join in. Her name was Lucy Lin. She was tall, beautiful, curvy and had long wavy brown hair. She still talked to me first thing in the morning, during the day and before the end of school.

'I warned you not to speak to Claire,' one girl told her. 'She's not good for you.'

Lucy would brush off the comment and kept talking to me. 'You know, you don't actually have to talk to me,' I told Lucy, but from the bottom of my heart, I felt like I was turning away my only friend.

'You don't deserve to be treated like this. It is not right, you didn't do anything wrong . Why do you just kept letting them spread the words and negative comments about you?' Lucy asked, looking at me with her big, beautiful brown eyes.

'I know I deserve better but Year 4 is going to end soon. It will get better,' I told Lucy. 'And I'm thankful you are willing to be my only friend. It's so painful that no-one wants to speak with me.' Not to mention how everyone was whispering when I passed.

The whispers and gossips became a nightmare that I often saw and heard when I was older, especially when I heard people talking or whispering to each other. It felt like they were gossiping or talking behind my back. That feeling and pain never really went away ... the criticism, judgement, hatred. I hid away at lunchtime to eat by myself and play volleyball on my own. Thankfully with Lucy next to me, I was able to 'get through' the whole year in less silence and pain.

When we moved into Year 5, people started to forget about the gossip and rumours. They started talking to me again, but now Lucy became the target for bullying and harassment. She had been gaining weight and getting pimples.

BEYOND BULLYING AND HARASSMENT

'Look at Lucy, she's so fat. Her face is disgusting. Her posture is so slumped.'

Suddenly everyone started avoiding her and wouldn't talk to her, but I refused to follow.

'This is ridiculous, just because she's different from us, you don't need to isolate her.'

I insisted on being by her side, being her only friend and being there for her no matter what.

It took a while for me and Lucy to let go of the 'lingering effects' of bullying and harassment. For a long time we stored the pain in our bodies – in our muscles (around the neck, shoulders and back), the gut, the chest and heart area, and around our face, head and fascia. Somatic psychotherapy was extremely helpful for both of us to encourage our bodies to process and release the stored tension.

> This story underscores the profound effects of empathy and resilience in confronting bullying. Lucy's kindness provided significant relief to me, and my support when she was targeted was a comfort to her. The lasting effects of bullying, including anxiety, persist into adulthood, but it is possible to break through the pain, especially when using body–based techniques to process the tension and pain stored in the fascia, muscles and organs.

> 'Bullying is not just about physical violence,
> it's also about psychological violence – the kind of violence
> that leaves scars on the soul.'
> – Julia Gillard

Mason heals his inner child

My client, Mason, came to one of our sessions after purchasing a breathing necklace and Peace Journal. He had endured significant harassment and bullying during his school years. Diagnosed at a very young age with the chronic skin condition vitiligo, characterised by depigmentation of portions of the skin, Mason faced relentless bullying from his peers. He was often mocked and cruelly referred to as a 'cow', 'zebra' and other animals. This verbal harassment and bullying led him to change schools multiple times, affecting his ability to settle into a stable environment. Despite these challenges, Mason persevered. He eventually completed high school and went on to graduate from university, where he earned a degree that enabled him to become an engineer at a prominent company.

By the time Mason sought my help, he was already doing quite well in many respects. He had worked extensively with psychologists and psychiatrists and had made remarkable progress in shifting many of his limiting beliefs and negative thought patterns. However, his main concern revolved around the lingering physical symptoms associated with anxiety. 'I still feel anxious and have these nightmares, night sweats and a "gutsy" feeling,' he explained.

His sessions began with the goal of resetting his nervous system. We focused on a specific technique designed to delve deep into the subconscious and connect with his inner child. This particular technique requires guidance throughout the process, providing instructions and observing him to ensure a safe and effective experience. The method induces a trance state, where sensations such as numbness, tingling or even pain might arise in the hands, feet or face. These physical sensations often signify the shedding of emotional layers, paving the way for the inner child to emerge.

As Mason progressed through these sessions, he had a profound realisation: 'I feel like it's not you who's going to help me heal, it's my inner child that's doing all the healing.' This acknowledgment marked a turning point in his healing journey. By consistently practising the exercises and engaging in regular follow-up sessions, we were able to address the deep-seated issues that had plagued him for years. Together, we unravelled layers of negative self-perceptions, including feelings of being 'not good enough', 'not lovable' and burdened by painful memories from bullying and mocking.

> With time, Mason began to experience significant improvements in both his mental and physical wellbeing. The combination of body-based techniques and targeted emotional healing provided him with the tools to navigate challenges at work and in life with greater resilience. His story is a testament to the transformative power of addressing the subconscious mind and inner child, highlighting the incredible capacity for healing that lies within each of us when guided with care and intention.

Melanie shakes off her past

Melanie came to me seeking help for the lingering effects of childhood bullying, which had left deep emotional scars. As a young girl, she had been vivacious and curious, but that spirit was dimmed when she became the target of relentless bullying. The torment began in primary school, where her classmates mocked her appearance and made cruel comments about her weight. By the time she entered high school, the bullying escalated to include exclusion, nasty rumours and occasional physical intimidation. The words 'fat', 'ugly' and 'useless' haunted her, becoming part of her self-perception. These experiences led Melanie to withdraw socially, struggling with self-esteem and feelings of worthlessness.

Even as an adult, Melanie found it challenging to shake off the effects of her past. She'd built a successful career as a graphic designer, but her personal life was often overshadowed by anxiety, self-doubt and a fear of rejection. She described feeling a constant 'knot' in her stomach and a tightness in her chest, particularly in social situations or during moments of vulnerability. 'I've worked with therapists before,' she told me, 'and while I've come a long way mentally, my body still feels stuck in the past. It's like I can't fully let go.'

To address her concerns, we focused on body-based techniques aimed at reconnecting Melanie with her sense of safety and wholeness. One of the foundational practices we introduced was a method designed to help individuals process and release trauma stored in the body. Trauma often becomes trapped within the nervous system, manifesting as chronic tension or a sense of being on high alert. This customised technique involved gently guiding her to tune into her physical sensations and gradually release the pent-up energy associated with traumatic events.

During our first session, Melanie described feeling an intense heaviness in her chest and a churning sensation in her stomach. I guided her to take slow, intentional breaths while focusing her attention on those sensations, together with deep tissue and trigger point release of the muscles. As we worked through the exercises, she began to notice subtle shifts in her body – the tightness in her chest eased slightly, and the churning in her stomach settled. These small victories built her confidence and trust in the process.

In subsequent sessions, we incorporated grounding techniques, movement and tactile exercises. Melanie found it helpful to place her feet firmly on the ground and visualise roots extending deep into the earth, providing her with a sense of stability and support. We also used a technique called pendulation, which involves alternating between focusing on areas of discomfort and areas of comfort or neutrality in the body. This helped Melanie build resilience and learn how to self-regulate when triggered.

Over time, Melanie experienced a profound transformation. The physical symptoms of her anxiety diminished, and she began to feel more present and confident in her daily life. One of the most powerful moments came during a session when she expressed gratitude to her younger self: 'You've been through so much, but you're still here, still standing.' This acknowledgment marked a turning point in her healing journey.

> By integrating body-based techniques with her existing emotional work, Melanie was able to release the residual sh*t and reconnect with her innate sense of worth. She now approaches life with a renewed sense of empowerment, knowing that she has the tools to navigate challenges and embrace her authentic self.

'Each of us deserves the freedom to pursue our own version of happiness. No-one deserves to be bullied.'
– Barack Obama

Why does bullying occur and what can you do?

People bully others for a variety of reasons, often stemming from their own emotional, psychological or social struggles. Five common reasons why people engage in bullying are:

1. **Insecurity or low self-esteem.** Bullies often feel inadequate or insecure about themselves and use bullying to assert dominance or mask their own vulnerabilities. Putting others down can give them a temporary sense of power or control.

2. **Past trauma or learned behaviour.** Individuals who have experienced abuse, neglect or bullying themselves may replicate these behaviours because it's what they've learned. They may view aggression as a way to cope with their own unresolved emotions.

3. **Desire for power or control.** Bullying can be a way to establish dominance in social or hierarchical situations. It may stem from a need to control others to feel important or superior.

4. **Social pressure or group dynamics.** In group settings, people may bully to fit in, gain approval, or avoid becoming a target themselves. Peer pressure can encourage individuals to engage in bullying behaviour to align with a dominant group.

5. **Lack of empathy or awareness.** Some bullies struggle to understand or care about the impact of their actions on others. They may lack emotional intelligence or have difficulty recognising the harm they cause.

So if you witness bullying, what can you do? Here are three steps you can take:

1. **Speak up and intervene:** If you witness bullying, step in safely to stop the behaviour. This could involve directly addressing the bully, supporting the victim or seeking help from an authority figure.

    Why it works: Speaking up shows the bully that their behaviour is unacceptable and helps the victim feel supported, reducing the bully's power.

2. **Create a supportive environment:** Foster an environment of inclusivity and respect in schools, workplaces and communities by promoting kindness, empathy and open communication.

Why it works: A positive culture discourages bullying behaviours and ensures that everyone feels valued and protected.

3. **Educate and raise awareness:** Provide education about the effects of bullying, why it happens and how to address it. This can include workshops, campaigns or conversations in schools, workplaces or communities.

    Why it works: Awareness empowers people to recognise bullying, understand its impact, and take appropriate action to prevent it. Education can also help potential bullies understand the harm they cause and encourage behaviour change.

By taking these steps, individuals and communities can work together to reduce bullying and create safer, more supportive spaces for everyone.

Healing self-practices to move beyond bullying

What does past bullying or harassment lead me to think about?
_____
_____
_____

How can I connect with my body more?
_____
_____
_____

What support can I get from the people around me?
_____
_____
_____

CHAPTER 6

Finding Hope in the Darkness

*The following content includes stories of suicidal thoughts that may be triggering. Please make sure you take care of yourself and seek support before you read, or you may wish to skip this chapter.

When I was 18, I struggled with depression and anxiety. I got into the best university, but I was not happy. I was actually dreading it. I seemed to have everything perfect on the outside, but deep down was an empty, sad and depressed soul.

I was very miserable, and when I was rejected by a guy that I liked, it felt like the last straw. With all this pressure coming from school, my parents, society, my peers, then on top of that, being rejected, I hit rock bottom and went to the school rooftop. I wanted to jump off and end my life.

But before I got to the edge of the rooftop, something stopped me. Something bigger stopped me from suicide. Afterwards, I started counselling and therapy, adding in spinal movement and breathwork. I began resetting my nervous system and my belief systems, and eventually I made a massive shift. A mixture of bottom–up and top–down approaches worked like a miracle. When addressing the pain stuck in our body and mind, we need a holistic approach to rewire our whole system.

When I think about the reasons I wanted to die at that point, I was experiencing a lot of pain and suffering. I thought if I end everything, things will be better. However, I did not necessarily want to end my life. I wanted to end the pain so I could end the suffering, mentally, physically and spiritually. But something stopped me, something held me back, and told me to ask for help, to seek support, to recover. Something told me that there was always hope.

From then on, I wanted to help people move better, to be pain–free, and that really changed my life and way of thinking. I don't think it was just my belief system – it was also my nervous system, my spiritual practices and the activities in my life.

I started doing the things I love. I went to drama classes and organised boot camps for high school students. I did more acting. I danced more. I ran the piano club. I started teaching Pilates. I started teaching breathwork. And all of that, it profoundly changed me because I found a way of living in my life. I found what brings me joy, what brings me happiness,

FINDING HOPE IN THE DARKNESS

what gives me a sense of purpose. It connected me to other people, and that connection to others really supported me in the long run. What I do is what keeps me going, what moves me forward.

And I encourage you to do that. I encourage you to find the ways, the things and the people that keep you going, that keep you moving forward, that help you put one foot in front of the other. That could be your purpose in life. It could be finding meaning in the things you do. It could be finding the communities and groups that truly support you and resonate with you.

> *'But in the end, one needs more*
> *courage to live than to kill himself.'*
> *– Albert Camus*

When we work on our belief system, it shifts our perspective, distorted thoughts and it feels less painful. As we work on our nervous system, our body feels more in control and has more energy. We feel more hope and less stress, overwhelm and burden. Connect with that joy and love for your body. Connect with movement, and also find your purpose.

James rediscovers his spirit

James, a 42-year-old former athlete, was battling depression after a career-ending injury left him unable to engage in the sports that once gave his life meaning. His physical pain was compounded by the loss of his identity, leading him to isolate himself. Eventually, he found himself filled with thoughts of suicide.

When James first came to me, his body language was as closed off as his emotional state. He slouched, held his arms tightly crossed and barely made eye contact. Recognising the deep connection between his nervous system state and his feelings, thoughts and behaviours, we began integrating body-based techniques into our sessions.

We started with simple questions to tap into the six states of his nervous system: hot, cold, flow, play, stillness and overwhelm state. Then we focused on the cold state, because this was where he was shut down, closed off, felt helpless and held all the thoughts around suicide.

We identified fire breathing as helpful breathwork to give him energy and strength to get through his day. He was able to regain his spirit and found his spirit animal through the session. This gave him the ability to control and create his new life, instead of living in despair and pain. He was also more in control over his thoughts, not staying stuck in overthinking and ruminating over the past mistakes and injuries he had.

James's injury left him with chronic back pain and hip pain, which often exacerbated his depressive symptoms. Through soft tissue release and self-massage, he learned to identify and release tension in his muscles. This not only helped alleviate his physical discomfort but also taught him a valuable metaphor: the release of physical tension mirrored the release of mental burdens.

Incorporating spinal movement helped him stretch and release fascia that stored a lot of trauma within his body. He felt a sense of accomplishment and progress and was able to connect his body and mind, allowing him to experience joy and freedom again, a critical step in rebuilding his self-esteem.

During sessions, we used guided imagery and visualisation to help James envision a life beyond his current pain. This technique helped him construct positive future scenarios where he was active, healthy and engaged with life.

Months into his sessions, James remarked that he no longer felt trapped in his body. His posture improved, his pain decreased, his smiles came more easily, and he started to engage in social activities again. While the journey was gradual, the integration of body-based techniques provided him with the tools to reclaim his life.

> By integrating body-based techniques with James's existing work with a psychologist, he was able to bring his spirit back to his body, release the sh*t he had stored and reconnect with who he was. Now James is ready to create a life of his own, let go of the baggage and move beyond his past and failures.

Sarah releases her stress

Sarah, a 35-year-old IT manager, faced relentless workplace stress and a series of personal losses that led her to a state of chronic anxiety and depression. Her coping mechanisms of smoking and drinking didn't work anymore and she began contemplating suicide as her only escape.

From our first session, it was clear that Sarah's mental turmoil manifested physically – she had persistent digestive issues, tight shoulders and frequent headaches. To address both her emotional and physical symptoms, we integrated body-based techniques into her sessions.

We began with somatic experiencing to help Sarah develop awareness of her bodily sensations associated with stress and trauma. This technique allowed her to 'track' her sensations and understand how her body held and responded to stress, providing insights into how to manage her reactions.

We then introduced mindful movement exercises to help Sarah reconnect with her body in a non-judgemental way. These exercises included walking meditations and gentle dance movements that emphasised presence and self-compassion.

As Sarah became more comfortable with bodily awareness, we introduced trauma release exercises, which involved specific exercises targeted at the muscle groups that held her pain and tension. This was particularly effective in reducing her physical symptoms, which were directly tied to her emotional state.

Over time, Sarah reported a significant decrease in her suicidal thoughts. She found new strength in her ability to manage her body's responses to stress. The power of integrating body-based healing techniques allowed her to envision a future filled with hope and resilience.

> Sarah's struggles manifested physically, resulting in digestive issues, tight shoulders and frequent headaches. Body-based techniques such as somatic experiencing, mindful movement and trauma release exercises helped her track and manage her body's stress responses. These interventions significantly reduced her physical symptoms and suicidal thoughts, empowering her to regain hope and resilience.

'When you don't have the strength to take another step, ask those you love to pull you.'
– Unknown

Understanding suicide

The desire to die by suicide is often complex and deeply rooted in overwhelming emotional pain, mental health challenges or feelings of hopelessness. People do not choose suicide lightly; it is often a desperate attempt to escape suffering that feels unbearable or inescapable.

It's unfair to tell someone you know you don't want them to die because their family or friends are going to be so sad or people are going to miss them. That is not a fair way to put it, even though it could feel like the truth. For the person who is wanting to die, they are unable to think about other people rationally, because at that point, their pain is so excruciating and overwhelming.

Some of the reasons people might want to choose suicide include:

- Mental health disorders: Conditions like depression, anxiety, bipolar disorder and PTSD can distort thinking and amplify feelings of hopelessness, despair or worthlessness. These disorders often leave individuals feeling trapped, unable to see solutions or believing they are beyond help.

- Hopelessness: A pervasive belief that life will never improve, problems are insurmountable or the future holds no joy or purpose can make suicide feel like the only escape.

- Social isolation and loneliness: Feeling disconnected or unsupported by friends, family or community can intensify feelings of invisibility and abandonment. Lack of meaningful relationships or a sense of belonging often contributes to suicidal thoughts.

- Trauma or abuse: Experiencing physical, emotional or sexual abuse, bullying, neglect or other forms of trauma can lead to shame, self-blame and a desire to escape the emotional pain. Unresolved trauma is a common driver of suicidal ideation.

- Chronic pain or illness: Persistent physical pain, terminal illness or debilitating health conditions can make life feel unbearable. The loss of independence or quality of life often contributes to thoughts of ending one's suffering.

Healing self-practices to find hope

*If you or someone you know is struggling with suicidal thoughts, it's important to seek help immediately. Support is available through crisis hotlines, mental health professionals and trusted individuals in your life. You are not alone, and recovery is possible.

1. Practise self-compassion. Recognising that suicidal thoughts are a symptom, not a personal failing, can help reduce shame and guilt.

2. Talk to someone or seek professional help. Reaching out to a trusted friend, family member or professional can help break the cycle of isolation. Seek professional help from therapists, counsellors and crisis lines, people who are trained to provide support and resources.

3. Create a safety plan. Identifying coping strategies and people to call in moments of crisis can be life-saving.

Creating your safety plan

It's important to recognise warning signs. Identify personal thoughts, feelings or behaviours that signal you're in a crisis. For example: feeling hopeless or overwhelmed, thinking 'I can't take this anymore' or withdrawing from friends or family.

HOW TO GET OVER YOUR SH*T

Write down your warning signs:
1. _____
2. _____
3. _____

Uncover some coping strategies that work for you. List healthy activities or techniques that can help you distract yourself or manage distress without needing someone else immediately. For example, listening to calming music or a favourite podcast, journalling your thoughts, taking a walk or engaging in light exercise.

Write down your coping strategies:
1. _____
2. _____
3. _____

Reaching out to trusted people is essential when all feels lost. Identify friends, family or loved ones you can talk to when you feel distressed. Let them know in advance that you may reach out during difficult times.

- Name: _____ | Phone: _____
- Name: _____ | Phone: _____

Contacting professionals or helplines can be really beneficial when you are struggling. List local or national crisis lines and mental health professionals you can call for immediate support.

- Therapist: _____ | Phone: _____
- Suicide crisis line: _____ | Phone: _____
- Emergency services: _____ | Phone: _____

CHAPTER 7

Loving Your Body

I struggled a lot with my body. My mother's self-hating language became mine, and all the shame, guilt and pain she felt became part of me. Every day she stood in front of the mirror, she always seemed to be struggling, to be angry at what she saw.

I didn't feel beautiful, lovable or comfortable in my skin. I didn't feel safe in my body. So often I just sort of dissociated. I left my body. When my mother looked at me, she was furious. She wanted my breasts to be two sizes bigger so they would look better. 'What happened to your breasts? I've fed you with so much milk, melon and papaya? I told you not to play those sports or lift weights,' she would say, not only disappointed in my body but also disappointed in hers. 'I made you into a C cup and now you drop down to B?'

I hated my uneven skin tone, my mouth, my nose, my eyes. At 14, I wanted plastic surgery. I wanted to change everything about me. I thought if I did surgery, everything would be better. I would be loved. I would be looked after.

When I was with a group of people, I'd find myself just floating over the top, dissociating from the actual place. In my head, I would ask myself so many questions, like, 'What am I supposed to say? How am I supposed to act? What do people think about me? What if they judge me?' I would just go down a rabbit hole. I was never really present. I was there in body, but my mind was not there. My spirit was not there. Then, everything changed when I was in Jyväskylä, Finland.

I arrived in Helsinki in the peak summer season. Finnish technical college had an exchange program with my university in Taiwan (National Yang Ming University) and I had the privilege to do my physiotherapy internship in Finland. I was thrilled and excited since I'd never been to the Nordic. At that time of year, the sun never goes down. Jyväskylä was 3 hours from Helsinki, in the middle of nowhere. It was a university town with a lot of international students and scholars. The midnight sun could have felt restless and overpowering, but it felt exciting and refreshing to me. I was somewhere else, doing something different from what I was used to, surrounded by lots of fascinating people.

The first few weeks were more like a holiday. I was settling in, discovering the town, trying to immerse myself in nature, exploring the lake and the woods as much as I could. To me, Jyväskylä was a peaceful escape from the hustle and bustle, unlike anywhere else in the world. It's full of international people, but in the middle of a Scandinavian land. A tucked away paradise, where you could connect and hang out with people from all over the world. For someone who came from a large city, Taipei, with over 2.64 million people, I fell in love with the country town immediately.

I was invited to join the sauna with my physiotherapy mentor, Määria. I was totally unaware that this involved getting naked in the shower and in the sauna with my teacher. We were facing each other in the shower while she explained hydrotherapy to me, and I did not know where to look because I was so uncomfortable. In the end, I learned to stare straight into her turquoise eyes and sometimes to her blonde short hair. It was all too new and odd for me.

The Finns are always naked in the sauna, to keep it as clean and pure as possible. Swimwear is not permitted due to the potential of lingering chemicals from pools evaporating in the heat. Also, with the heat up to 80–100 degrees, it can affect the synthetic materials on the swimwear. Not even a towel is permitted inside. It usually takes people from overseas some time to get used to this tradition.

I sat in the sauna not just with Määria, but with Eevä–Liisa as well, another Finnish mentor. A lot of times we sat in there and chatted about business, clients or culture differences. In the beginning, I really felt like hiding my body. I would wrap my arms around my top and hope that they were not judging my breast size or broad shoulders. However, the more I sat in these sessions, the more comfortable I became.

The sauna has been an integral part of Finnish culture for centuries. It is a place for business, connection, social and network purposes. It was everywhere – in the clinic, at the school, at the swimming pool, in every office building, in every home, on the rooftop. In the sauna, you get naked and really open about different things. It's also a place where families, friends and communities gather to relax, bond and engage in meaningful conversations. It became my daily routine when I was in Finland, especially after gym exercises. I would sit in the sauna for recovery. It was healing and sacred, and helped me renew my body image and confidence. I saw many types of bodies, breasts and buttocks in the sauna and became accustomed to the variety and beauty of humans.

> *'Until you love yourself, you will never know who you really are and you won't know what you are really capable of.'*
> *– Louise Hay*

It felt so good being naked and I felt so comfortable being around people that didn't judge. People came into the sauna and just carried on with the conversation. They didn't really look around or start gossiping or judging, because they started using a sauna when they were three or four, and they're used to being in the zone. And you get used to it too. You get used to being part of a culture where everyone is naked and so comfortable. That was something I really loved about being in Finland, because it gave me the love that I have for my body. It rebuilt my body image and my confidence.

LOVING YOUR BODY

I was hanging out with my friends after sauna near the Finnish Lakes. We loved jumping in and out of the sauna and lake to help us recover.

Sonia heals her body image

Sonia is a beautiful girl from Hawaii. She has ADHD, depression and anxiety. She struggled a lot with her body image and used extreme measures to control her diet and exercise. She was forced to change her diet because of a gut problem, and cut down on gluten. She was seeing a psychic medium when we met and was doing tarot cards and oracle cards daily to ease her uncertainty and anxiety.

When she came to me, she was just out of a very toxic relationship. After breaking free, she didn't see any psychologist because the traditional cognitive behavioural therapy (CBT) hadn't really worked for her. Her anxiety stemmed mostly from childhood and adulthood sh*t and her nervous system did not allow her to process them on a conscious level. She often felt insecure and uncomfortable in her own body. She didn't feel safe or at ease within herself, and told me, 'I hate my body and I don't like the way I look.'

We started to reset her nervous system, firstly trying to understand where her flow state and her connected state is. We could see it had shrunk because of the traumatic events that happened in the past. Once we mapped that out, we mapped out her fight/flight state and freeze state. She got into a fight/flight state when she stood in front of the mirror, and shut down when she saw other couples where the woman seemed more beautiful than herself. It reminded her that she's not worthy of love and desire.

When she stood in front of the mirror, thoughts came up, such as, 'Oh, you are just so ugly. You are not skinny enough. Your boobs are too small.' Those thoughts went through her mind.

We explored various techniques to help her stay within her body, because she didn't feel safe to do so. She often dissociated from her body, which is a mechanism the body does to protect itself. In a way, that was safe in the past, where she could run away from the traumatic events that happened that were related to her body, but it was not helpful for her living in the moment.

This type of technique requires a specialised body practitioner to be next to the client to gently bring in the proprioception of the body. During our sessions, we brought in three techniques to help the body to return to a calm state. This combination helped Sonia stay in her body when triggers occurred. She was more aware of her 'shut down' state and was able to use those techniques to come back to her body. Once the trauma layers shed, her body felt safe, and she felt more comfortable in her own skin. She finally felt at home.

We also created a plan for her to spend time in nature – not just walking fast or listening to podcasts, but intentionally connecting. I encouraged her to feel the grass under her feet, describe the sensations of walking barefoot, and notice the feelings on her skin, the air, the smells and the sounds around her.

By engaging all her senses in nature, she began to reconnect with her body. This practice gave her the autonomy to observe what was happening within her body and her internal system. It supported her healing because, when people experience trauma, their interoception (their ability to sense internal bodily states) often changes. It becomes harder to feel sensations, emotions, or safety within themselves.

This approach helped Sonia tune into her body more deeply. I guided her to reflect on areas that felt harder to connect with, asking questions like:

- Are there parts of your body that feel harder to connect to?
- What feelings are present there?
- Do any stories or beliefs arise about these sensations, such as 'my shoulder is broken' or 'I am broken'?

By connecting from head to shoulders, down the spine, to hands, belly, pelvis, knees and feet, she practised observing her body holistically. If a part felt hard to connect with, like her stomach, I encouraged her to notice what that felt like, the thoughts that came up, and how her energy shifted after completing the exercise.

This daily practice builds body awareness and mindfulness. Paying attention to our bodies in nature makes us better at regulating and resetting our nervous systems. It helps us understand and connect with ourselves on a deeper level.

'I feel like the surrounding is so real and authentic. I feel like I am really in my own body. I am no longer abandoning my body or dissociating to avoid the pain,' Sonia shared.

> By practising the exercise daily and catching up on a weekly basis to work through the challenges Sonia faced with her body, we were able to resolve the layers of shame, guilt and pain around her body. It was not about how fast or quickly she improved. The key was that because she kept coming back to her body, she began feeling safe in each moment. Anything that Sonia does, or any choice or decision that she makes in the moment, she is able to make the right decision at the right moment – for herself, not out of fear or stress. She's able to make decisions that feel safe and secure. She's able to move forward with her business.

LOVING YOUR BODY

Noah accepts her body

Noah's journey to self-love and acceptance began after years of struggling with her body image. Growing up, she was constantly bombarded with messages that her body wasn't good enough. From a young age, she endured emotional abuse from her family, who would criticise her weight and appearance. These negative comments became the lens through which she viewed herself, and she grew up believing that her worth was tied to how closely she fit society's ideals.

As a teenager, Noah turned to social media for comfort and inspiration. She became captivated by curvy celebrities who exuded confidence and embraced their bodies. Figures like these gave her a glimmer of hope that she, too, could love herself one day. However, the more she tried to emulate them, the more she felt like she was falling short. The curated perfection of their lives made her hyper-aware of her own flaws, and she struggled to reconcile her body with the images she admired.

By the time Noah reached her twenties, the toll of years of self-criticism was evident. She avoided mirrors, wore baggy clothes to hide her shape, and declined social invitations out of fear of being judged. 'I felt like I was invisible,' she later said. 'Or maybe I wanted to be invisible. It was easier than facing the world.'

Noah's turning point came when she attended one of my workshops. At first, she was sceptical. The idea of celebrating her body felt impossible. But as she listened to others share their stories, she began to see a common thread: they had all felt unworthy, yet they were learning to embrace themselves despite societal expectations. It was the first time Noah realised she wasn't alone in her struggle.

Inspired by the workshop, Noah decided to explore more body-based renew practices with me. She began with mindful movement, starting with gentle spinal exercise where she could reconnect with her body in a safe and supportive environment. For the first time, she started to appreciate her body for what it could do rather than how it looked.

Specific breathing techniques also became a cornerstone of her recovery process. Noah learned to release the tension and shame she'd been holding in her body for years. During one session, she experienced a powerful emotional release and cried heavily as she realised just how much she'd internalised other people's opinions about her worth.

As Noah continued her journey, she also shifted her relationship with social media. Instead of following accounts that made her feel inadequate, she curated her feed to include diverse, body-positive creators. Seeing people of all shapes and sizes celebrate themselves helped Noah reframe her perspective. She began to see her own body as unique and beautiful.

> As months turned into years, Noah's relationship with her body transformed. She started wearing clothes that made her feel good, looked in the mirror with kindness, and even began sharing her own journey on social media to inspire others. 'For the first time, I see my body for what it is: strong, resilient and beautiful,' she said. Noah was able to tap into self-compassion and redefine beauty on her own terms.

LOVING YOUR BODY

'Look into a mirror, make eye contact with yourself, and say "I love me" as many times as possible during the day.'
— Wayne Dyer

Connect to the rhythm of life

The natural environment, whether it's the lake, the ocean, the forest or the mountains, is all about harmony. Everything operates in sync, and that sense of connection helps calm our minds, bringing us relaxation and peace.

I loved the nature in Finland. It was beautiful, so serene and calm. I spent a lot of time in the Finnish forest. It was everywhere, surrounding my apartment. In just 10 minutes I could be immersed in its peace and beauty. I usually spent around half an hour in the evening walking in the forest. I liked this best in the cold dark winter, just to enjoy the crispy snow and coldness under my shoes, and the quietness and serenity of the woods. It gave me a sense of peace, and time to reflect and think about the things that happen in life.

The relationship between nature and people in Finland is beautiful. The Finnish truly love nature, and they leave it as it is meant to be – very true to itself. I spent a lot of time walking, hiking and skiing in the forests. In the summer, we often visited an island near the school. We took a boat, rowed it ourselves and enjoyed the sun with some wine and sangria on board. We also took time to sit on the grass, play volleyball, talk to each other, and have barbecues and picnics. Time in nature feels so full of love. That is why it has such a healing power. I truly believe nature has the power to heal.

When we are in nature, we are more connected to ourselves. It aligns us with the rhythm of life. Nature is simple and balanced – forests, lakes and even the smallest elements all operate in harmony. That flow and connection calms our minds, bringing us relaxation and peace.

Being in nature also lowers cortisol, the stress hormone we carry daily. Just walking in the forest, sitting by the lake, or swimming in the water activates the parasympathetic nervous system, helping the body rest and recover. When our nervous system is in a heightened state (like when we feel we're fighting or fleeing from a situation) getting closer to nature can help. Whether it's a forest, a lake or even just being around greenery, it helps to regulate our system.

Nature offers so many different sounds and sensations: the waves, rustling leaves, blooming flowers, chirping birds and vibrant colours. These invite us to fully engage our senses, drawing us into the present moment. Nature makes me feel like I'm truly in the moment and grounded in my body. It feels safe, calm and secure to be within myself, and that's incredibly important.

Being in nature also exposes us to sunlight and fresh air, which are healing. Sunlight gives us vitamin D, essential for our mood and immune function. Scheduling time in nature is an excellent way to regulate the nervous system, stay present and be grounded.

One practice I recommend (even though I'm not the biggest fan of doing it myself) is called grounding or earthing, which is simply walking barefoot on grass or sand. It connects us physically to the Earth's energy, helping discharge negative energy from past triggers or pain. Grounding can reduce inflammation, relieve pain, improve sleep and promote overall wellbeing. This is why I encourage my clients to visit the ocean, lake, forest, park or even just a tree, at least once a week. It helps to regulate your nervous system, align you with natural rhythms, reduce stress and reconnect you with your body.

> I know for some, it can be challenging to be around nature. So here is a meditation that you can also check out online (https://breatheintopeace.com/products/forest-meditation). It is a meditation in the forest that will guide you to feel more connected to your body, more connected to your senses and the present moment. This meditation will help you to be more grounded and present if you just need a short break in between work.

Why we don't love our bodies

Many people nowadays don't like their bodies, especially women. Some common reasons why we don't like our bodies include:

- Unrealistic beauty standards from the media and societal ideals promote unattainable definitions of beauty, making people feel they fall short
- Comparison with others, especially on social media, leads to feelings of inadequacy
- Negative self-talk or harsh inner criticism about our appearance can fuel body dissatisfaction
- Past trauma or criticism from experiences like bullying,

body shaming or critical comments from others can leave lasting scars
- Health or physical changes due to aging, weight gain or loss, illness or other factors can make people feel disconnected from their bodies.

Healing self-practices for loving your body

When did I first start feeling dissatisfied with my body, and what triggered it?

_____
_____
_____

How would I view or treat a loved one who has similar body features as me?

_____
_____
_____

What are some things my body allows me to do that I'm grateful for?

_____
_____
_____

CHAPTER 8

Reclaim Your Power

I blinked twice and couldn't believe my eyes. *This is happening to me! This is ridiculous! What would people say about this!* I was once scammed A$20,000 and it was an overwhelming, sad and depressing experience for me, because I didn't see it coming. I thought someone so smart, independent and strong would never get scammed.

I was at work when the scammer called, and they mentioned they were an IT company that's checking cybersecurity of the company. There was something wrong with my laptop and I'd been exposed. They said they will take care of it but they need access my laptop. I blindly just followed the instructions step by step, and the next thing I knew, I lost $20,000. My account went from $20,000 to $0 in just 5 minutes!

Eventually after 2 months, I claimed the full amount back from the bank because the bank had missed an important security step. After that, I swiftly changed banks. This experience taught me that mistakes can happen to anyone – and that there are always ways to get yourself out of the sh*t that happened.

After this, I decided I had to move out of my two-bedroom house, where I lived by myself. I explained the situation to my real estate agent and luckily my lease was about to end. I moved into another house with others who I felt comfortable and connected with. I found it easier to be surrounded by people so I was not always in my head, indulging in the negative thoughts and negative situations. My nervous system was definitely in the freeze and shut down state. I was feeling hopeless, helpless and very depressed and sad. I knew deep down that this state was not going to help me, that my body was trying to protect me by doing nothing or simply shutting down.

I pulled out the paper that listed my 'feel-good activities'. It's something I prepared and carried with me always. On the paper I had written specific activities that will help me move to boost my energy and mood. As I practised some of the activities over the days and weeks, I started to move out my depressed state. My energy level would shift from low to high, but I still felt despair, sadness and disgust. Even though the negative energy and unpleasant feelings remained, I could feel myself moving up the scale.

When you find yourself stuck, that's what you need to do – move. Find activities or things that help you move out of that helpless and hopeless state.

RECLAIM YOUR POWER

I started focusing on the tasks and activities that I truly enjoy doing, like writing, walking and swimming. In our lowest moments, we need those activities to ground us and shift us to a state that's slightly better. Even if it's temporary, that's okay. We won't always stay there forever, but it's worth remembering that the pleasurable activities we have on hand can help shift our energy, emotional state, and ultimately, our wellbeing.

As strange as it sounds, after I was scammed, I rediscovered those activities that bring me joy. Slowly but surely, I began feeling better and taking action to reclaim what was lost. At the same time, I developed this deep sense of appreciation for myself. I realised just how amazing I am and how much I truly value myself. This came from my daily practice of brain-down and body-up approaches. They helped me see through the challenges and find ways to tackle them head-on. That self-appreciation didn't happen overnight. It has been years in the making, doing the deep inner work.

Now, every morning I wake up, look in the mirror and say, 'I love you.' I follow it with affirmations that remind me of my strength and worth. And I want you to remember this: it's possible for you too. It's possible for any of us to wake up feeling proud of ourselves – proud of who we are and who we're becoming.

'Mistakes are a fact of life.
It is the response to the error that counts.'
– Nikki Giovanni

> Life can throw unexpected challenges our way. But when we cultivate strong self-love and compassion, we're able to bounce back so much faster. Uncover some activities to bring love and joy into your daily or weekly routine. Learn to appreciate yourself, give yourself compliments and express gratitude for who you are. It's a powerful practice that I hope you carry with you. I love you, and I want you to love yourself too.

Jessica learns to love herself

Jessica's journey to self-love was one of courage, reflection and transformation. For years, she struggled with feelings of inadequacy and self-doubt stemming from a series of personal and professional mistakes. Each misstep seemed to reinforce a narrative that she wasn't good enough. She often ruminated over past decisions, such as leaving a stable job to pursue a passion project that failed, or ending a relationship she later felt could have been saved. These thoughts kept her stuck in a cycle of regret and self-criticism.

By the time Jessica sought help, she was determined to break free from this pattern. Together, we worked on integrating both brain-down and body-up approaches to address her challenges holistically. The brain-down approach focused on reshaping her thought patterns, while the body-up approach concentrated on reconnecting with her body and her belief system to process stored emotions.

Through the brain−down approach, Jessica began cognitive restructuring. She learned to identify and challenge the negative beliefs that had taken root in her mind. For example, when she caught herself thinking, 'I always mess everything up,' we reframed it to 'I made a mistake, but I am learning and growing from it.' This shift in mindset was reinforced through journalling exercises where she recorded her progress and celebrated small wins. Over time, Jessica started to see her mistakes not as evidence of failure, but as opportunities for growth.

Simultaneously, we implemented the body−up approach to address the emotional impact of her past experiences. Jessica's body often carried the weight of her self−criticism in the form of tension, particularly in her shoulders, chest and back. To release this, we used somatic techniques to move the tension out of the body. In one session, Jessica engaged in extensive breathing exercise while moving her thoracic and lumbar spine. As she allowed herself to feel the tightness without judgement, tears began to flow as she felt the release. 'I didn't realise how much I've been holding in,' she said. This release marked a significant step in her healing process.

Spinal movement also became a valuable tool for Jessica. It helped her reconnect with her body in a positive way, fostering a sense of gratitude for its resilience. She began to appreciate her body not for how it looked, but for how it supported her every day. This newfound connection strengthened her ability to process emotions and remain present in the moment.

As Jessica progressed, she integrated the lessons from both approaches into her daily life. In just 5–10 minutes each day, she moved her body and practised self−compassion through affirmations and continued journalling her thoughts and feelings afterwards. When she felt overwhelmed, she turned to body–up techniques that would ground her as she went about her day.

> Over time, Jessica's perception of herself transformed. She began to see her past mistakes as stepping stones rather than setbacks. 'I've learned that loving myself means embracing all parts of me – the wins and the losses,' she reflected. Finally, she is able to truly accept and love herself.

'You need to give yourself permission to be human.'
– Joyce Brothers

What is an emotion matrix?

The emotion matrix is a conceptual tool used to map, understand and analyse emotions based on specific dimensions or factors, such as intensity, pleasantness (positive or negative) and arousal (high or low). It helps in visualising how different emotions are related and how they impact on behaviour and decision–making.

RECLAIM YOUR POWER

Enraged	Panicked	Stressed	Jittery	Shocked	Surprised	Upbeat	Festive	Exhilarated	Ecstatic
Livid	Furious	Frustrated	Tense	Stunned	Hyper	Cheerful	Motivated	Inspired	Elated
Fuming	Frightened	Angry	Nervous	Restless	Energized	Lively	Enthusiastic	Optimistic	Excited
Anxious	Apprehensive	Worried	Irritated	Annoyed	Pleased	Happy	Focused	Proud	Thrilled
Repulsed	Troubled	Concerned	Uneasy	Peeved	Pleasant	Joyful	Hopeful	Playful	Blissful
Disgusted	Glum	Disappointed	Down	Apathetic	At ease	Easygoing	Content	Loving	Fulfilled
Pessimistic	Morose	Discouraged	Sad	Bored	Calm	Secure	Satisfied	Grateful	Touched
Alienated	Miserable	Lonely	Disheartened	Tired	Relaxed	Chill	Restful	Blessed	Balanced
Despondent	Depressed	Sullen	Exhausted	Fatigued	Mellow	Thoughtful	Peaceful	Comfy	Carefree
Despair	Hopeless	Desolate	Spent	Drained	Sleepy	Complacent	Tranquil	Cozy	Serene

← Low Pleasantness   High Pleasantness → (High Energy ↑ / Low Energy ↓)

This is an emotion matrix where you can identify how you are feeling and how you are going to move out of those emotions.

Common dimensions in an emotion matrix include:

- Pleasantness: represents how pleasant or unpleasant an emotion feels.
    - Positive emotions: joy, excitement, fun
    - Negative emotions: sadness, anger, despair

- Arousal: indicates the level of energy or activation associated with an emotion.
    - High arousal: anxiety, euphoria
    - Low arousal: calmness, boredom.

This is a great tool to help you be more aware of your emotions, triggers and state and find ways to regulate them better. I highly recommend you identify where you fall emotionally in a given situation and develop strategies to shift your feelings toward a more desired state.

What is an affirmation?

An affirmation is a positive statement or declaration that you repeat to yourself, often to encourage self-belief, motivation or emotional wellness. Affirmations are used to influence your thoughts and behaviours by focusing on empowering and optimistic thoughts.

The purpose of affirmations are to boost confidence, change negative thought patterns and support emotional wellbeing. Here are some examples:

- 'I am capable and confident in achieving my goals.'
- 'Every day, I am becoming healthier and stronger.'
- 'I deserve love, respect and success.'
- 'I am grateful for the abundance in my life.'

How to use affirmations

1. Repetition: Say them daily, preferably in the morning or before bed.
2. Belief: Choose affirmations that feel meaningful and believable to you.
3. Visualisation: Picture yourself embodying the affirmation as you say it.
4. Consistency: Regular practice helps rewire thought patterns over time.

Healing self-practices for reclaiming your power

How am I feeling now? What are the emotions I am experiencing?
_____
_____
_____

What activities can I do to shift my energy from low to slightly higher?
_____
_____
_____

How can I shift my pleasantness?
_____
_____
_____

CHAPTER 9

Breaking Free from Abuse

I met many boys during my time living and travelling across Europe. I spent time in the Czech Republic, Spain, Switzerland, Finland, Sweden, Russia and the Baltic Sea and I had a lot of fun. My intention was to explore the world. At that time, I didn't think much about the encounters or the swift intimacy; it just happened naturally. These experiences made me start rethinking the differences between men and women – how we view our bodies, intimacy and relationships very differently.

This reflection made me wonder if I was ready for something more profound, meaningful and serious. With that thought in mind, I returned to Finland and settled into my second year living there. That's when a friend introduced me to Otto. He was Caucasian, very tall and ruggedly masculine. He studied IT engineering, had a daughter, and had won several fencing competitions. On the surface, he seemed perfect.

We spent a lot of time together and got to know each other. I was drawn to his maturity, physique, and toughness in work and life. Yet, deep down, my gut told me something wasn't right. Despite my instincts, I stayed with him. Over the next few months, things turned abusive.

At first, it started during intimacy. We engaged in bondage and other adventurous practices, which we both enjoyed. However, he began to hit me during these moments. Over time, the violence escalated outside the bedroom. Arguments would lead to him grabbing me, hitting me, shouting and swearing. It went downhill from there. He began seeing other women, including my friends, while still with me.

The relationship was toxic from the beginning, but I allowed myself to stay. He often brought up my childhood trauma, saying things like, 'Do you love me because I'm like your father? Because I beat you like your family did?' It was devastating.

Breaking free wasn't easy. We shared intense sexual chemistry and an addictive attachment. Our dynamic was intoxicating and provocative. But I knew I had to leave. To help myself, I blocked him on all social media and wrote down all the reasons why he was not good for me. This process gave me clarity and determination.

We had only been together for 12 months, but the damage was immense. Writing about our time together, month by month, documenting the abuse, helped me see the pattern clearly. I realised how little I knew him, despite how intense everything felt initially.

To heal, I immersed myself in friendships and activities like gym workouts, hikes and skiing. Spending time with others and shifting my focus helped me rebuild. Observing the relationship from a neutral perspective allowed me to understand the abuse, manipulation and mockery I endured. He had belittled my appearance, laughed at my skin colour and degraded me in countless ways.

> *'You're in relationship to be happy, to smile, to laugh and to make good memories. Not to be constantly upset, to feel hurt and to cry.'*
> *– Anonymous*

As a coach and practitioner, I've worked with many women who've experienced abusive relationships. A recurring theme is the connection between their upbringing and their relationship patterns. Women with a history of neglect or abuse, whether emotional, physical or mental, often find themselves in familiar cycles with partners. Trauma shapes the nervous system, narrowing the window of tolerance and making unhealthy dynamics feel 'normal' or even 'safe'. Despite gut feelings warning them, many women stay because the abuse feels familiar, like home, even though it's far from healthy, safe or comfortable. These women often struggle with anxiety, boundary-setting and speaking up. Their abusers are often intertwined in their lives, making it harder to escape.

I spoke on stage at Sydney International Convention Centre about building mental resilience by resetting the nervous system. I've also spoken at Melbourne Convention and Exhibition Centre, conferences and corporate events.

Simone breaks free from toxic relationships

Simone, my dear client, faced a similar situation in a toxic, narcissistic relationship. Her partner's behaviour had left her feeling drained, confused and questioning her own worth. To help her gain clarity, I encouraged her to document every instance of mistreatment in her relationship. Writing down each incident, whether it was neglect, verbal abuse or physical harm, made it clear how toxic her partner was. The act of writing served as a mirror, reflecting back the reality she had been enduring.

One of the hardest but most crucial steps for Simone was detaching herself from the social circle connected to him. These were people who either enabled his behaviour or were too entwined with the relationship dynamics to provide genuine support. Letting go of these connections was painful, but it opened the door for her to build a new, healthier community. Gradually, Simone began to surround herself with people who uplifted her and encouraged her healing.

Simone also practised body–based techniques to address the physical and emotional toll of her relationship. Many of these techniques were aimed at calming her heightened nervous system, which had been in a state of constant fight–or–flight. From various customised techniques, she learned to regulate her body's responses to stress. These practices became her anchor during moments of anxiety or when memories of her partner's behaviour resurfaced. Each session focused on boosting her self–worth and confidence, which she strengthened through repetition. Whenever she felt triggered, Simone turned to these exercises to ground herself and regain a sense of control.

Setting boundaries proved to be the hardest part for Simone. Years of being in a toxic relationship had eroded her ability to say 'no' or assert her needs. We started small. She practised saying 'no' to minor requests – declining an invitation if she didn't feel like attending or ignoring social media connections that didn't serve her wellbeing. As she gained confidence, Simone expanded her ability to assert herself, gradually stretching her comfort zone and reclaiming her power. Each time she stood her ground, her nervous system adapted, reinforcing her newfound sense of empowerment.

Eventually, Simone reached a point where she could confidently say 'no' to toxic individuals who pursued her. Whether it was a manipulative friend or a man with red flags, Simone learned to trust her instincts and prioritise her wellbeing. The transformation was profound.

> Today, Simone is thriving. She's single, but she's happier and more fulfilled than ever. Surrounded by supportive friends and pursuing her passions, she's created a life that reflects her values and celebrates her growth. Simone's story shows that it's possible to get out of abusive relationships, heal from the pain and find light at the end of the tunnel.

*'Overcoming abuse doesn't just happen,
it takes positive steps every day. Let today be the
day you start to move forward.'*
– Assunta Harris

What is an abusive relationships?

An abusive relationship is a dynamic where one person exerts power and control over another through harmful behaviours. Abuse can manifest in various forms, including:

- Physical abuse: Hitting, slapping, choking or any form of physical violence intended to hurt or intimidate the victim
- Emotional abuse: Manipulation, criticism, humiliation, gaslighting or other tactics that harm a person's self-esteem and emotional wellbeing

- Verbal abuse: Yelling, name-calling, insults or threats designed to intimidate, belittle or control the victim
- Sexual abuse: Forcing or pressuring someone into sexual acts without consent, or using sex as a weapon to dominate or punish
- Financial abuse: Controlling a person's access to money, sabotaging their ability to earn income or using finances to manipulate and restrict their independence
- Psychological abuse: Using fear, threats or intimidation to control another person, often making them feel trapped or powerless.

Signs you may be in an abusive relationship

- You feel scared or anxious about your partner's reactions.
- Your partner constantly criticises or belittles you.
- You feel isolated from friends and family because of the relationship.
- Your partner monitors your movements, communication or finances.
- You've been threatened or hurt physically or emotionally.
- Your self-worth has decreased since entering the relationship.

Abusive relationships often leave the victim feeling trapped, confused or responsible for the abuse. However, the abuse is never the victim's fault. Seeking help from trusted friends, family or professionals is a critical step towards breaking free and healing.

Why do some people engage in casual relationships? (aka f**kboy or playgirl)

People engage in casual relationships for various reasons, mostly it has nothing to do with the other person. Some reasons might include:

- Fear of commitment: they avoid emotional closeness or long-term obligations due to anxiety, fear of vulnerability or past heartbreak
- Need for validation: seeking attention from multiple partners boosts their self-esteem or fills emotional needs
- Cultural or social influence: societal norms, peer pressure or status associated with casual relationships encourage this behaviour
- Attachment or emotional detachment: avoidant attachment styles or struggles with emotional intimacy lead them to prefer surface-level relationships
- Exploration or avoidance of responsibility: they may use casual relationships to explore, avoid settling down or evade the responsibilities of commitment.

Healing self-practices to break free from abuse

How do I feel when I am in this relationship or friendship?
_____
_____
_____

If I identify that I am in an abusive relationships, what are the patterns of toxic behaviour?
_____
_____
_____

What steps can I take to get out of this relationship?
_____
_____
_____

CHAPTER 10

Uncover Your Success

When I moved to Singapore, I was starting fresh in my career. Initially, I taught Pilates, but I soon transitioned into physiotherapy at a prestigious clinic, working with clients experiencing chronic pain. It felt like a dream job, an opportunity to grow after my time in Europe.

Arriving in Singapore, I was determined to build a successful career. My clients were working in banks and law firms and were lovely, and my colleagues were decent. But I quickly learned an essential skill: asking for what I want. If I wanted to focus on pre– and postnatal clients, I asked. If I wanted to visit doctors in hospitals or clinics to collaborate, I asked. And when you're clear and prepared, more often than not, you get what you ask for.

Of course, challenges arose. In one of my early group classes, a pregnant client felt the exercises were unsafe and asked for a refund. My boss had to intervene, offering her a free session with another therapist. That experience led to a discussion with my boss about improving my approach, teaching me how to reflect and adapt. Another time, a client complained about body odour. The clinic manager kindly suggested I use a different deodorant. While such moments were humbling, I accepted them as opportunities to grow. Over time, I became one of the clinic's most sought-after therapists. My schedule was fully booked, and clients experienced significant pain relief and improved quality of life.

This journey taught me that asking for what you want and being open to feedback are crucial for growth. Whether it's a salary review, a new role or a performance discussion, it's important to communicate your desires. Timing and preparation matter – approaching the right person, with a clear ask, at the right moment, ensures you're taken seriously.

My experience in Singapore wasn't just about career advancement. It was a lesson in building relationships and connections. This applies to business as well: before making an ask, focus on giving value and establishing trust. Whether pitching to an event organiser, collaborating with influential people, or offering a product, building rapport makes the 'ask' more natural and effective.

While I was working as a professional in Singapore, my Australian manager recognised my skills and talents in selling. I'm one of those physiotherapist who would personally rock up at the hospital or clinic to talk to doctors and specialist to tell them about our services. I don't get hurt with nos or rejections. I simply knock on the door and go in and ask.

I would even invite doctors to come into the clinic for free sessions. The confidence was always there. It might have something to do with my childhood selling experience (remember the pizza and soft drink?). Selling was fun, thrilling and exciting for me. I didn't have much attachment to the outcome of sales. For me, it was about connecting with people, sharing what we do and inviting people in.

Eventually, my workdays were split, so I did 3 days in business development and 3 days seeing private clients or teaching group classes. I'm grateful for the opportunity because it showed me the world outside the traditional therapy room. When I got into business development full time later in Australia, I cut down my clinical hours from 15–20 hours to 3 hours per week. It was a big change, and saying goodbye to private clients was hard. However, I love sales because it's unpredictable; you never know what is going to happen. In seeing private clients, I know if they follow the protocols, follow the home exercises and keep up with regular check-ins they will usually progress after a set amount of sessions. But sales is different. You don't know who will be interested in your products or services. There are assumptions, but the reality can be quite different. I love the testing phase, and just putting the service or product out there and see who is interested and who might be buying.

> 'Ask for what you want and be prepared to get it.'
> – Maya Angelou

> I'm always grateful for what I learned in Singapore, from negotiation and closing deals to managing a team. It really helped me set the foundation for my business, and is transferable to any work that I do in the future.

Amy's dream becomes a reality

One of my clients, Amy, had a dream: she wanted her unique art candles to be sold in airport shops, showcasing her creativity to travellers from all over the world. However, the path to achieving this dream wasn't immediately clear. Amy felt unsure and overwhelmed at first, uncertain how to turn her vision into reality.

That's when she decided to start with visualisation. Every day, Amy spent time imagining her candles displayed prominently in the stores, envisioning travellers admiring her work, and hearing compliments from customers, store managers and even art enthusiasts. This practice wasn't just about daydreaming, it gave Amy the confidence and focus to move forward. By vividly experiencing the feelings of excitement, pride and accomplishment in her mind, she began to believe her vision was achievable.

With her confidence bolstered, Amy took tangible steps toward her goal. She collaborated with a talented First Nations artist to add a unique cultural dimension to her candles, making them even more special. She also polished her product catalogue to professional standards, sent it to key buyers, and set up meetings with store managers. Amy knew that persistence was key, and she continued to align her actions with her vision. Eventually, her hard work paid off, and her art candles made it into airport shops, exactly as she had visualised.

Amy's journey is a perfect example of how dreams, no matter how big or distant they may seem, can become a reality when broken into actionable steps. By embodying the emotions of success – confidence, joy and enthusiasm – she created the momentum to keep moving forward. It wasn't about controlling the outcome but about staying aligned with her vision and trusting the process.

This story highlights a powerful truth: ownership of your career or business is essential. Reflect on what makes you unhappy and identify what could bring you joy or fulfillment. Often, the feeling of being 'stuck' is just a mindset. It's fuelled by overthinking or procrastination, but the way out is simpler than we imagine – small, consistent actions can create incredible shifts.

For instance, if you love public speaking, start by taking small opportunities within your company or community. A single event can lead to another, building confidence and creating a network of growth and possibilities. That's exactly how I started my own speaking journey. I began with local events, which led to speaking at business conferences, and eventually, I found myself on stage at major festivals like the MindBodySpirit Festival, Spark Festival and gift trade shows, sharing my message with hundreds of people.

Amy's story – and mine – proves that progress is all about small, intentional steps. Each step builds on the last, creating momentum and bringing you closer to your goals. Success isn't about taking massive leaps, but about consistently moving forward, even when the path feels uncertain. Each step builds confidence.

> If you're ready to take ownership of your dreams, start today. Visualise your goal, feel the excitement of achieving it and take the first small step. Like Amy, you'll find that with persistence and alignment, your vision can become your reality.

'Your imagination is your preview
of life's coming attractions.'
– Albert Einstein

Taking ownership of your path

In business, success often begins with asking. It could be asking an event organiser for a chance to speak on stage, reaching out to a potential customer for a conversation or inviting influential people to try your products or services. However, it's crucial to build a relationship first. I believe in focusing on creating a genuine connection before making any requests.

I wouldn't approach things coldly; instead, I'd invest time in understanding and connecting with the other person. Once the relationship is established, asking becomes easier. This approach has worked consistently for my clients and me. I often suggest a 'give, give and then ask' strategy. By giving first, by sharing your values and demonstrating your impact, you set the stage for a successful ask. When people see the value and outcomes you bring, they are far more likely to say yes.

This approach was instrumental when I incorporated First Nations art by Gary Purchase into our stationery collection. Gary, an award-winning artist from the Central Coast, creates stunning works inspired by spirit animals like whales, which are displayed in shopping malls, train stations, schools and more. His success is a testament to how First Nations artists can thrive in today's landscape.

When I started this project, I reached out to several First Nations artists, prioritising relationship-building over immediate outcomes. Not every ask was successful, but eventually, we partnered with Gary because it felt aligned – both of us value mental health and resilience. This synergy made the collaboration meaningful and impactful.

Confidence and clarity also play a significant role in asking for what you want. These qualities often come from taking action. Overthinking can keep us stuck, but action gives us feedback and direction. For instance, when I pursued speaking engagements, I discovered how much I enjoyed it. By doing, not just thinking, I honed my craft, gained confidence and created opportunities. Over time, speaking became a positive cycle: the more I spoke, the more I improved, and the more opportunities came my way.

I encourage my clients to take bold steps, even if they're afraid. Whether it's making that intimidating phone call or sending a message, action creates momentum. Manifestation also plays a part in this journey. Visualisation, reframing and strategic action can align your desires with reality. For example, I vividly imagined myself speaking at the Bondi Beach Club, feeling the audience's enthusiasm and support. I embodied every detail – what I saw, heard and felt – and eventually, that vision materialised. Visualisation doesn't guarantee exact outcomes, it creates a pathway toward them by aligning your actions with your goals.

If you feel stuck remember, being stuck is often a mental state, not a physical reality. Take small steps – say hello to a colleague, ask for opportunities that excite you, or tackle a challenge that scares you. These small actions compound, creating momentum and leading to opportunities you may not have anticipated. The key is to keep moving forward. Focus on what brings you joy and growth, and don't be afraid to ask for the life and career you want. Success is a series of small steps, not a single leap.

What is manifestation?

Manifestation is the practice of intentionally bringing your goals, desires or dreams into reality by focusing your thoughts, emotions and actions in alignment with what you want to achieve. It's based on the idea that your mindset and energy can influence the outcomes in your life. While it often involves spiritual concepts, many people also view it as a tool for goal setting and achieving clarity.

To practise manifestation, there are several steps to follow:

- Clarify your desires: be specific about what you want to manifest. Write it down in detail, for example, 'I want to feel confident and land a six-figure job by

December next year.' Ask yourself: *Why do I want this? How will it make me feel?*
- Set a positive intention: use affirmations or clear statements in the present tense to express your desire as if it's already true. For example, 'I am thriving in my dream job with confidence and ease.'
- Visualise your goals: spend a few minutes daily imagining yourself already living your dream life. Engage all your senses. What does it look, feel, or sound like?
- Feel the emotions: focus on the emotions tied to achieving your desire (e.g. joy, gratitude, excitement). These emotions raise your energy and make you more aligned with what you want.
- Take inspired action: manifestation isn't just about thinking positively. Take tangible steps toward your goals while trusting the process.
- Release doubt: Trust in the timing and let go of obsessing over the outcome. Worry and doubt can block the manifestation process.

Manifestation is most powerful when combined with personal growth and actionable steps. It's about aligning your imagination, emotions and actions to bring your dreams into reality. Visualisation is a powerful tool, but it must be paired with consistent action. Amy, for example, wanted to see her indigenous art candles displayed in airport shops. Through visualisation exercises, she embodied the feeling of success, imagining her products in stores and how it would feel to achieve that goal. This clarity gave her the courage to take action, contacting store managers, sending catalogues and setting up meetings.

The journey to success is rarely linear. It's about taking small, consistent steps, learning from setbacks and staying open to growth.

Healing self-practices to uncover your success

What do I want to manifest in my career or business?
1. _____
2. _____
3. _____

How do I bring that into my visualisation? Lean into the 5 senses.
1. I can see _____
2. I can feel _____
3. I can hear _____
4. I can smell _____
5. I can taste _____

What inspired action can I take today to move forward with this goal in mind?
_____
_____
_____
_____

CHAPTER 11

Breaking Free from Toxic Environments

When I was working in Singapore, I was in a high-end clinic with all the luxury brands, when my mentor Alice started to ask me to do things I didn't want to do, like picking up her lunch or taking her washing to the laundromat. She was a great mentor; she could have really helped me develop my skills in therapy. But it gave me a lot of stress and anxiety when I had to speak with her. She was always picking up small things that weren't right with the exercise or the tools I offered. And she asked me all these favours that were outside of my work. From time to time, I had to look after her clients, and after a few sessions, they did not want to return to her as 'her clients'. Alice got upset, and thought I was stealing her clients.

A colleague, Chloe came to me and shared that Alice was actually a bully. 'She kept asking me to do things, and now she's doing the same to you,' she said.

Cora also came and told me about some of her clients. After a few 'cover' sessions when Alice was away, none of them wanted to return to her. 'Alice is harsh on her clients. If the clients are 10 minutes late, then she would be 10 minutes late as well to see the clients. So in total, in the end, the clients missed 20 minutes of the session,' Cora explained. 'And sometimes she deliberately chose challenging exercises to make the clients uncomfortable. It wasn't just about helping them get better but purposefully defeating them, making them feel inferior, and that didn't feel nice. So when they got a chance to work with other therapists, they chose to move.'

In a way, I was lucky that I had colleagues who were open to sharing their experiences and their situations with me. I understood that it wasn't just me who was facing the bullying or harassment, that there were other people experiencing this as well. Sometimes, it can be hard to know if you are in a toxic workplace or around a toxic person, especially if you had an abusive past. It is challenging to identify what is normal and what isn't, since our nervous system could be dysregulated already. At first, we think it is normal. We tolerate it, agree to it, but the fact is, it isn't normal. You do not need to tolerate or agree to it. You can stand up for yourself or leave the place.

My employer in Singapore, Dylan, had very high expectations. He gave me a heavy workload with unreasonable deadlines. I worked 6 days every week, teaching Pilates and seeing physiotherapy and visiting corporate clients. Eventually, I experienced burnout and an injury, and couldn't go to work. I had to pause for 2 months. During this period, Dylan became really aggressive and angry. He and the clinic manager sent messages and asked about my sick leave, personal leave and hospital leave. Some of the messages that came through included: *'Are you pretending to be sick? Were you trying to get injured so you could take a break or rest? Are you trying to get money out of the company?'*

These messages were really, really disheartening and very hurtful. I hadn't expected my workplace to become toxic. My doctor prescribed 2–3 months off. I was already depressed from the injury. I felt like I was useless. I felt hopeless, helpless and unsure if there was any hope in my work and life. I wanted to find a way to come back.

One thing that really helped me was finding a community and a circle of friends that gave me a different energy. When we are depressed, we want to shut down, do nothing and in a way, our bodies are trying to protect us. We may feel like nothing is worth doing, as though everything around us is black and grey. We might lose the desire to engage with anything. It affects how we feel, how we think and how we behave. This sadness wasn't temporary, it was persistent, ongoing and overwhelming. I experienced hopelessness, emptiness and deep sadness that seemed endless. I felt worthless, guilty and constantly criticised myself.

Fortunately, I met Tina, who introduced me to her group of friends. Through behavioural activation, I started connecting with new people and participating in social activities. These experiences slowly began to shed light on my life. I started to see hope. I began to feel a little more content, a little happier and more interested in trying new things. Over time, I started to feel worthwhile again and began praising myself instead of criticising.

One memorable day, Tina dressed me up in a beautiful kimono, and we attended the horse races together. Her friends took photos of us, and we enjoyed sitting in the lounge, eating delicious food and drinking Japanese alcohol while watching the races. Despite wearing a knee brace and wrist brace at the time, I felt beautiful. I felt a sense of hope and joy and light amidst everything I'd been through.

> *'Leadership is not about being in charge. It's about taking care of those in your charge.'*
> *— Simon Sinek*

> These social interactions and moments of co-regulation gave me the energy to move forward, to keep thriving. I was so grateful to Tina for helping me overcome challenges and empowering me to stand up for myself.

Me and my friends in kimonos at the races.

BREAKING FREE FROM TOXIC ENVIRONMENTS

Julie's struggle in a leadership role

One of my clients, Julie, was an operations manager in a telecom company. When her company underwent leadership changes, the culture turned toxic. Gossip, poor communication and a lack of support left her feeling undervalued and eventually led to burnout.

Julie found herself lying in bed, her body unwilling to get up for work. She called me one morning, saying she might have experienced burnout. Together, we went through the symptoms of burnout, which included headaches, stomach-aches, fatigue and exhaustion. She also felt helpless, cynical and entirely unmotivated. She described feeling detached from the world, as though it was closing in on her. Over time, she began withdrawing and isolating herself from her work colleagues, retreating into her own space as the stress became overwhelming.

We discussed how burnout might stem from a stressful work environment or taking on too many responsibilities. It often emerged from prolonged exposure to chronic stress or pressure. Julie's nervous system had been constantly stuck in a fight-or-flight state, oscillating between those and the freeze state. She had reached a point where she could no longer sustain the energy required to perform at her usual capacity.

To help Julie recover, we crafted a 5-step plan to address the root causes of her burnout and restore her wellbeing. These steps were intentional and designed to rebuild her mental, emotional and physical resilience.

First, we worked on acknowledging the burnout and creating space for her feelings without judgement. Julie admitted that she often ignored her own needs and pushed through her limits. Recognising this pattern helped her accept that she needed to slow down and prioritise her recovery.

Next, we focused on setting boundaries at work. Julie learned how to delegate tasks effectively and say no to additional responsibilities that would push her beyond her limits. This was particularly challenging at first, as she worried about being perceived as weak. However, with practice, she began to notice that her colleagues respected her boundaries and even admired her assertiveness.

The third step involved reconnecting with activities that brought her joy. Julie rediscovered hobbies she had neglected, such as painting and walking. These moments of creativity and mindfulness provided her with a sense of accomplishment and relaxation, helping to counteract the stress she had been experiencing.

We also incorporated techniques to regulate her nervous system, customising them to support her when she entered a fight, flight or freeze state. These practices allowed Julie to shift out of those modes and into a calmer, more balanced state.

Finally, Julie began rebuilding her social connections. She reached out to trusted colleagues and friends, fostering supportive relationships that provided her with a sense of belonging and encouragement. Sharing her experiences with others also helped her feel less alone in her struggles.

> Over time, Julie started to feel a renewed sense of purpose and energy. By taking intentional steps to recover, she regained her confidence, rediscovered her motivation, and began leading her team with resilience and clarity. Her journey showed that recovery from burnout is possible with the right support and tools.

Mark learns to say no more often

Mark, a registered nurse with years of experience, had always been passionate about his work. Helping patients to recover and providing comfort during difficult times gave him a profound sense of purpose. However, his role had become increasingly demanding under a manager who seemed to prioritise efficiency over the wellbeing of the staff. The relentless demands, tight deadlines, and frequent overtime shifts were beginning to negatively impact his physical and mental wellness.

Mark felt trapped. Each day he pushed through exhaustion, driven by guilt over leaving his colleagues short-staffed or letting his patients down. But the mounting pressure was affecting him in ways he couldn't ignore. He found himself irritable at home, snapping at loved ones and dreading every shift. His sleep suffered, and the physical fatigue he experienced was mirrored by an emotional numbness. He began to question whether he could continue in a profession he once loved.

One evening, after a particularly gruelling double shift, Mark broke down in frustration. He knew something had to change but felt powerless to address the situation. That's when he knocked on my door and asked me how to regain control over his life. In private coaching sessions, Mark learned to regulate his emotions and approach conversations with calm confidence. I showed him how to focus on slow exhalation breathing techniques, which became a daily practice, helping him find clarity, and slow down his heart rate and breathing, even in high-pressure moments. Equipped with these new tools, Mark decided to address the situation with his manager directly.

The conversation was nerve-wrecking. Mark had rehearsed his points, focusing on the facts rather than his emotions. He described the challenges he faced, explaining how the unreasonable workload was affecting his ability to provide the level of care his patients deserved. Mark expressed his concerns calmly but firmly, and for the first time, his manager seemed to listen.

The turning point came when Mark referenced the hospital's policies, emphasising the importance of nurse recovery time between shifts. He wasn't confrontational but instead focused on how a more balanced schedule would benefit everyone, from the staff to the patients. To his surprise, his manager acknowledged the validity of his points and agreed to review the scheduling practices.

In the weeks that followed, Mark noticed a significant improvement. His shifts became more manageable, and he finally had time to rest and recharge. With the weight of constant exhaustion lifted, he began to rediscover his passion for nursing. He no longer felt like he was just surviving each day but instead thriving in a career that he loved.

Beyond the changes at work, Mark experienced a deeper transformation. Learning to advocate for himself and manage stress taught him that he didn't have to accept conditions that undermined his wellbeing. He realised the power of setting boundaries and speaking up, not just for himself but for the quality of care his patients deserved.

> Mark's journey wasn't just about resolving workplace issues; it was about reclaiming his sense of self. The process reminded him that even in the most challenging circumstances, it's possible to find solutions and rediscover joy and purpose.

'Toxic people are like a piece of gum stuck to your shoe. They're sticky and annoying, and they refuse to let you go.'
— *Anonymous*

What is a toxic workplace?

Workplaces with unrealistic expectations, like high workloads, tight deadlines, a lack of boundaries or disrespectful behaviour, can quickly become toxic. Issues like micromanagement, bullying, gossip, misinformation, manipulation or even high turnover can create a culture of negativity, blame and conflict where trust is eroded. Unfortunately, 80% of the Australian workforce reports experiencing some level of toxicity. This is why, whenever I speak at events about workplace dynamics, people often feel triggered or upset. It brings up traumatic memories tied to their work environments.

Many workplaces can push employees into survival mode, creating fear and anxiety. That's why I encourage you to evaluate your current work environment or even your own business. Ask yourself if it's fostering a safe, respectful and healthy space. Does it offer realistic expectations, minimal micromanagement, fairness and growth opportunities?

The first step is awareness – identifying whether your workplace is toxic. With this baseline, you can decide whether to try and influence change or leave for a healthier environment. Remember, changing workplace culture is often challenging, as it starts with leadership. Regulated, emotionally stable leaders create calmer and more emotionally supportive workplaces. Conversely, reactive, high-stress leaders often cultivate teams that mirror this survival-state behaviour.

It's important to consider speaking with others in your team or workplace about the situation, but ensure that the conversation remains respectful and confidential between the involved parties. Sometimes, though, you may need to escalate the matter to your HR manager or a senior leader, like your CEO, especially if it's seriously impacting your wellbeing.

If you're not in a position to influence leadership, it may be best to find a workplace with a positive culture, one that prioritises respect, balance and opportunities for growth.

Introducing DEAR MAN

One skill I learned during my time in a toxic workplace was a communication strategy called DEAR MAN. This tool helped me effectively express my needs and wants, especially

BREAKING FREE FROM TOXIC ENVIRONMENTS

during a difficult period when I was receiving threats, judgement and criticism from my managers and directors. Using DEAR MAN, I was able to set boundaries and have assertive conversations with my employer. This skill became a vital part of my journey towards reclaiming my voice and strength.

The DEAR MAN technique is a valuable tool for navigating difficult workplace dynamics. Here's how it works:

D – Describe: Clearly and concisely outline the facts without judgement. For example: *'You've asked me to work past 9 pm three times this week.'* Focus solely on the facts.

E – Express: Use 'I' statements to share your feelings. For instance: *'I feel overwhelmed and anxious due to the extra hours.'* Be honest about your emotions.

A – Assert: State your needs clearly and specifically. For example: *'I need to resume my regular 40-hour workweek and finish work by 6 pm.'* Refer back to your employment contract if needed.

R – Reinforce: Reward positive responses. A simple *'Thank you'* or a smile can acknowledge their understanding and encourage future cooperation.

M – Mindfulness: Stay focused on your goals and avoid being derailed by unrelated issues. For example: *'I'd like to resolve the overtime issue before discussing new projects.'*

A – Appear confident: Use body language to project confidence, even if you don't feel it. Stand tall, make eye contact and avoid fidgeting. Believe in what you're saying, and others will too.

N – Negotiate: Know your limits and be prepared to compromise where appropriate. For example: *'I can work late tonight, but I won't be available past 6 pm moving forward.'* Clearly state what you're willing to accept.

5 steps to burnout recovery

Burnout recovery is a gradual process that requires commitment to self-care and lifestyle adjustments. By taking these five steps, you can regain energy, clarity and fulfillment while building mental wellness and mental resilience to navigate challenges more effectively in the future.

Step 1: Recognise and acknowledge the burnout

- Identify the symptoms: Be honest about how burnout is affecting you emotionally, mentally and physically.
- Accept your state: Acknowledge that burnout is a valid condition and not a sign of failure or weakness. This step is critical to move towards healing.
- Reflect on the causes: Understand what has contributed to your burnout (e.g. work stress, lack of boundaries, personal pressures).

Step 2: Prioritise rest and recovery

- Take immediate breaks: Step away from demanding tasks, even if temporarily, to reduce stress.

BREAKING FREE FROM TOXIC ENVIRONMENTS

- Focus on sleep: Ensure you get 7–10 hours of restful sleep each night to recharge your body and mind.
- Engage in relaxing activities: Practise mindfulness, meditation, Pilates, breathwork or hobbies that bring joy.

Step 3: Reassess your priorities and boundaries

- Define what matters: Identify the core values and goals that truly resonate with you.
- Set boundaries: Say no to tasks or responsibilities that overwhelm you, and protect your time and energy.
- Simplify your life: Delegate or eliminate non-essential tasks to create space for recovery.

Step 4: Rebuild with support

- Seek social connection: Talk to trusted friends, family or colleagues for emotional support and perspective.
- Consult professionals: Work with a therapist, counsellor or coach to explore coping strategies and deeper healing.
- Join support networks: Engage with groups or communities that understand and address burnout.

Step 5: Create a sustainable lifestyle

- Develop healthy habits: Incorporate regular exercise, nutritious eating and daily relaxation techniques into your routine.
- Balance work and life: Allocate time for work, rest and play, ensuring a well-rounded schedule.
- Commit to self-care: Regularly check-in with yourself and prioritise activities that nurture your wellbeing.

- Adopt resilience practices: Cultivate skills like stress management, adaptability and nervous system reset to prevent future burnout.

Healing self-practices to address a toxic workplace

Practising DEAR MAN is highly effective, but it can feel daunting at first, especially if it triggers anxiety or feels outside your comfort zone. Breaking it into smaller steps can help.

Start by describing and expressing your feelings in simple scenarios.

_____
_____
_____

Gradually add more detail, asserting your needs and reinforcing positive behaviour.

_____
_____
_____

Listen to and observe feedback from other people.

_____
_____
_____

BREAKING FREE FROM TOXIC ENVIRONMENTS

Setting boundaries may cause discomfort like fast heartbeats, sweaty palms or nervousness, but that's normal when building new habits. With practice, it becomes easier. Incorporating body–based exercises can help regulate your nervous system during these conversations.

If you're dealing with toxicity, whether at work, in relationships or within your family, I encourage you to start using DEAR MAN. It's a skill that empowers you to stand your ground, communicate effectively and build healthier dynamics.

CHAPTER 12

Letting Go of the Past

When I first relocated to Melbourne, I was determined to recover from rock bottom. My work visa was rejected in Singapore, so I had to leave everything behind. I chose to make a quick move to Melbourne since everyone recommended Australia. After I visited for 10 days, I was obsessed with the Great Ocean Road and the cold winter in Melbourne. I was hoping it would be a new opportunity to accept myself again. But at first, I was stuck in the past, replaying all the things I should have done differently, like booking the right tickets or arranging accommodations to avoid being sent back.

I lived in this state of regret every day. I was working as a Pilates instructor, helping corporate professionals and business owners relieve pain in their shoulders and backs, but my personal life was stagnant. After work, I'd go home and ruminate on my past – on my failures, toxic workplaces, abusive partners and traumatic childhood. Even my housemate noticed. They'd encourage me to go out or stop beating myself up, pointing out how much I was living in the past. But I didn't know if there was a way out.

My working visa allowed me to work with unique patient groups, those in specialised communities and nursing homes with chronic illnesses, mental health issues like anxiety, schizophrenia, bipolar and depression, or severe physical conditions. These patients lived in supported housing with 24/7 care, rarely seeing the outside world.

Initially, working with them was overwhelming. Many patients screamed, banged their heads against walls, or lived in their own realities, often repeating things endlessly. It was exhausting, and I thought about quitting so many times. Most of my Australian colleagues lasted only three days in these roles before leaving for less intense jobs. But I was a foreigner. I was new in Australia. I was determined to make it work.

The first lesson I learned was the importance of setting boundaries – energetic, emotional and physical boundaries. I began visualising a protective bubble around me, a bright white light that shielded me from negative energy. This bubble helped me stay grounded and protected me from the overwhelming emotions in the room. When I felt negativity leaking toward me, I imagined a transparent wall between myself and the patient. This wall allowed me to care for them while safeguarding my energy. These tools were lifesavers for maintaining my wellbeing while working with patients in such challenging circumstances.

LETTING GO OF THE PAST

Melbourne itself presented challenges. The unpredictable weather, shifting from storms to sunshine in minutes, reminded me of my own struggles with emotional regulation. My borderline personality disorder made me swing between intense excitement and deep rejection. It was during this time that I embraced rejection as part of life. Working with clients who often refused treatment helped me build resilience. I saw it as exposure therapy, starting small and gradually building tolerance. Over time, rejection lost its sting, preparing me for the realities of running my own product and coaching business.

By 2019, the pandemic hit. Life in Melbourne changed, and so did I. Walking along Altona Beach between client sessions, I found peace and clarity. I felt a deep pull toward something greater – a mission to help others with anxiety, those that are just like me. This marked the start of my entrepreneurial journey. With the extra time lockdowns gave me, I began learning about business and facing my fears head-on, like recording videos and posting online. At first, it was nerve-wrecking. I worried about being judged – what if my parents laughed at me? What if people thought I was a fraud?

But I pushed through, starting with 1-minute videos, gradually increasing the length to 15 minutes and even a 1-hour video, helping my nervous system adapt to the anxiety and stress. Over time, I became more confident and began sharing my story authentically. The shift came when I stopped trying to be perfect and focused on connection. I shared my journey of transformation from someone overwhelmed with anxiety to someone who was calm and at peace. My first authentic post in a Facebook group received over 400 likes and comments, proving that my story resonated.

This validation gave me the courage to continue. Soon, I attracted clients from all over the world, including New Zealand, the USA, Canada and across Australia. I started seeing coaching clients and helping others achieve breakthroughs. I also created breathing necklaces, journals and cards, to provide people with practical tools to support their mental wellness and resilience.

Building my business wasn't smooth sailing. There were triggers and challenges, but every obstacle became a growth opportunity. I realised business is like a spiritual journey, forcing you to face your deepest fears and grow. At every level, there's always a new challenge.

> *'Awareness is the first step in healing.'*
> – Dean Ornish

> Today, I've built a successful business, been featured on TV, podcasts and stages, and helped countless others transform their lives. I want to share this to show you that anything is possible. By shifting your perspective, healing your nervous system, and breaking free from limiting beliefs, you can overcome any challenge and create a life you love.

LETTING GO OF THE PAST

Here's me, being interviewed about 'Anxiety Relief' and 'Reset Nervous System' on TickerNews in March 2025. I've been dreaming about this moment for 5 years and it's finally came true.

Frankie breaks free from her past

Frankie had been carrying the weight of her past for as long as she could remember. Her life was shaped by the scars of complex trauma, leaving her feeling like she was perpetually stuck in an endless cycle of pain and struggle. Over the years, she sought counselling, hoping to find relief and answers. She went to session after session, talking about her problems, dissecting her pain, and searching for solutions. But the more she tried to fix herself, the more broken she felt. It was as if every effort to heal only uncovered new layers of wounds.

She often described feeling like a puzzle with missing pieces, convinced she would never be whole. 'Why am I always struggling?' she'd ask. It seemed like no matter how much work she put in, the pain persisted. Frankie was caught in the belief that if only she could solve all her problems, she would finally feel okay. But life kept presenting new challenges, and the endless pursuit of healing left her exhausted.

When she reached out to me after being referred by a friend, I suggested we take a different approach. Instead of talking about her problems, we would focus on her body. We began a practice of deeply conscious, connected bodywork, shifting the focus away from the mind and into her physical and emotional core. We tapped into her nervous system and explored the parts of herself that had been ignored, the parts that longed not to be fixed, but to be seen and felt.

As we delved into the session, something incredible happened. Frankie began to connect with her inner child – the part of her that had existed long before the trauma, the part that still carried innocence, curiosity and joy. For the first time in years, she wasn't consumed by the pain of her past. Instead, she started to see vibrant colours in her mind's eye, feel warmth in her heart, and experience a lightness she had forgotten was possible.

By the end of the session, Frankie emerged transformed. She was surprised by what she felt – happiness, satisfaction, and a deep sense of connection to herself. Tears filled her eyes, not from pain, but from a profound realisation: she was not broken. The narrative she had carried for so long, that she was damaged and in need of endless fixing, began to unravel. Frankie understood that her inner child, this vibrant and loving part of herself, had always been there, waiting to guide her back to joy and love.

LETTING GO OF THE PAST

Life, she realised, will always have its sh*t – its challenges and messes. But those struggles don't define her, nor do they take away her ability to feel joy and create happiness. Frankie felt empowered by the knowledge that even among the chaos and mess, she could tap into a deeper part of herself that was whole, resilient and alive.

The session wasn't a magic cure—all. Healing is a journey, not a destination. But for Frankie, this experience marked a turning point. She no longer felt like she was fighting to fix something broken. Instead, she began to embrace herself fully, knowing that she could hold both her struggles and her joy. That is the power of our nervous system – it has the ability to ground us, heal us, and reconnect us to the essence of who we are.

> When we work on the nervous system, it subconsciously uncovers hidden strength. It shows us we have the power to take control of the things that have shaped us. We can actually look at things differently. We can be proud of our inner child, proud of who we are, who we've become, and what we've chosen to be.

'Healing may not be so much about getting better, as about letting go of everything that isn't you – all of the expectations, all of the beliefs – and becoming who you are.'
– Rachel Naomi Remen

What does healing mean?

Healing is the process of restoring balance, peace and wholeness to our mind, body and spirit. It's not just about overcoming physical illness or emotional wounds; it's about creating a life where we feel empowered, present and aligned with our true selves.

At its core, healing means:

- Releasing pain: Letting go of the hurt, anger, guilt or resentment that weighs us down. It doesn't mean forgetting or dismissing our experiences, but allowing ourselves to feel and release them so they no longer define us
- Reconnecting with ourselves: Healing invites us to listen deeply to our inner voice, to honour our needs, and to nurture our sense of self–worth. It's about reconnecting with who we truly are beneath the layers of pain or trauma
- Transforming patterns: It means breaking free from cycles of thought, behaviour, or relationships that no longer serve us. Healing empowers us to step into healthier patterns that support growth and happiness
- Building resilience: True healing makes us stronger, teaching us to face challenges with grace and courage. It helps us trust in our ability to navigate life, no matter what comes our way
- Finding meaning: Healing is often about discovering purpose in our struggles. It's about turning pain into wisdom and using it to create a life that feels meaningful and fulfilling.

LETTING GO OF THE PAST

Healing is not a linear journey. It's messy, imperfect and deeply personal. It can involve counselling, therapy, self-reflection, resetting our nervous system, connecting with others, or practices like breathwork, spinal movement, dancing, eye movement, energy healing and spending time in nature.

Above all, healing is a commitment to yourself – a declaration that you deserve peace, joy and the freedom to thrive.

And I want you to remember this:

Your body is smarter than your mind. Our bodies are remarkable, intuitive systems that often hold wisdom far beyond what our conscious minds can comprehend. While our minds are filled with thoughts, beliefs and societal conditioning, our bodies operate on a primal, instinctual level, responding to the environment in real time and communicating truths that our thoughts might obscure.

One clear example of this intelligence is the nervous system. When faced with danger, your body automatically activates the fight, flight or freeze response without waiting for your mind to deliberate. Your heart races, muscles tense and adrenaline surges, preparing you to act. This happens faster than your conscious mind can even process the threat. Your body doesn't need you to 'think' your way to safety; it simply reacts to protect you.

Another area where your body's intelligence shines is in its ability to signal unmet needs. Have you ever felt a knot in your stomach before making a big decision or a tightness in your chest during a stressful situation? These sensations are your body's way of alerting you to internal misalignments. While your mind might rationalise staying in a job or relationship that doesn't serve you, your body will speak louder, manifesting unease, fatigue or even illness as it tries to get your attention.

Similarly, the body has an incredible capacity for healing. If you cut your finger, your body immediately begins clotting the blood, fighting potential infections and repairing the tissue – all without you needing to consciously intervene. Your immune system is constantly scanning for and addressing threats like bacteria or viruses, keeping you alive and well. This innate intelligence operates far beyond the scope of what your mind can control.

The body is also deeply attuned to emotional truths. Long before your conscious mind catches on, your body can sense when something feels wrong – or right. For instance, you might feel a warmth or lightness in your chest when you're around someone who uplifts you, or a sinking heaviness when you're in an unsafe or toxic environment. These physical sensations are often more accurate than the mental stories we tell ourselves.

Various research shows that trauma is stored in the body. You might consciously believe you've moved on from a painful event, but your body remembers. It may respond with tension, digestive issues or chronic pain, subtly urging you to address unresolved emotions. By learning to listen to your body and work through these sensations, you can release what your mind cannot rationalise away.

Your body's intelligence isn't separate from your mind, it's an integral part of who you are. By tuning into the sensations, signals and emotions your body provides, you can access deeper clarity and alignment than your thoughts alone could ever offer.

Trusting your body is trusting yourself. Because your body holds profound wisdom.

Healing self-practices for letting go of the past

What do I want to release from my past?
_____
_____
_____

Which part of me do I want to connect with the most?
_____
_____
_____

What are some of the tools I can use to get better?
_____
_____
_____

CHAPTER 13

Flourishing in New Beginnings

In 2021, I moved to Sydney. I had grown tired of Melbourne, even though I love the city deeply. Melbourne holds a special place in my heart because much of my personal healing happened there. Despite the gloomy weather and the introverted vibe of the people, it was in Melbourne that I started to co-regulate with others and embrace my authentic self. I learned to speak up and express myself genuinely.

During the pandemic, Melbourne faced some of the strictest lockdowns in the world, with 254 days of restrictions out of 365 in 2020. It was a challenging time for everyone. To cope, I started swimming in the cold ocean, often under the cover of darkness to avoid curfews and the strict 5 km travel rules. This act of rebellion wasn't about breaking rules but about finding solace and connection during an isolating time. With gyms, salons, restaurants and most businesses shut, the city felt eerie and lifeless. Many of my friends faced devastating losses. Some had to close businesses, while others declared bankruptcy or were forced to change careers.

For me, the lockdown was tough but manageable. I had already developed a good relationship with my anxiety and depression. I stayed connected with friends, met new people and found joy in cold ocean swims, sometimes even under the full moon. These small moments of connection brought a sense of normalcy, but the overall experience left a lasting impression of gloom. When Melbourne reopened, it didn't feel the same. The energy of the city had shifted, and I no longer felt at home there. I decided to move to Sydney. At the time, I still had my house in Melbourne, but I didn't overthink it. I just knew Sydney was where I needed to be.

My love for Sydney began in 2020 when I visited for work. Driving through the city's lush green suburbs and tranquil seaside neighbourhoods, I felt an instant pull. Sydney offered a different kind of vibrancy, one that resonated with my evolving self. While I had always thought of myself as a 'Melbourne girl', someone who appreciates culture, coffee, theatre and comedy, I realised Sydney's beaches, greenery and entrepreneurial energy aligned more with the life I wanted to create.

Sydney is expensive, with houses at the time ranging from $1.2 million to upwards of $20+ million, and apartments starting at $700,000. While basic living costs like food and transportation are similar to Melbourne, extras like gym memberships and salon visits can be pricier, largely due to higher rents. But Sydney offers something invaluable: opportunities. The city thrives on innovation, encouraging startups and new ventures, which made it the perfect place for me to take Breathe Into Peace to the next level.

Interestingly, while most of our business partners and clients are still in Melbourne, moving to Sydney allowed me to focus on addressing something deeper: my relationship with money. This was crucial to my growth as a business owner. Growing up, money was a source of stress in my family. Both my parents were academics, but they constantly worried about finances. This scarcity mindset left a lasting imprint on me, creating a broken record of constantly 'not having enough'. I carried this belief into adulthood, always feeling like my earnings and success weren't enough. Even as I achieved milestones in my business, I found myself focusing on what I lacked rather than appreciating what I had. This mindset nearly drove me to bankruptcy.

The turning point came when I began healing my money trauma. I recognised the old narratives I was holding onto, like my dad's words during a family shopping trip in the US: 'Stop buying, we're going broke.' Even though it wasn't true, this statement echoed in my mind for years, shaping my fears around money and success. To move forward, I started shifting my beliefs and practising gratitude for the abundance already in my life. I created daily habits, like writing a 'receiving list' to acknowledge every opportunity, client and act of kindness that came my way. I reframed my thoughts, choosing affirmations like: *'I am a magnet for opportunity. Today, I choose to welcome abundance.'*

I also used music as a tool to shift my energy, creating playlists that inspired feelings of prosperity and joy. These small but powerful practices helped me embody confidence and attract new opportunities. In just two weeks, I closed $10,000 in sales, followed by another $15,000 in the next month, giving my business the momentum it needed. (I go deeper on Nervous System Reset & Sales Flow https://breatheintopeace.com/products/salesflow)

> 'Even the greatest was once a beginner.
> Don't be afraid to take that first step.'
> – Muhammad Ali

For any entrepreneur, especially those struggling with feelings of lack or scarcity, it's vital to address these underlying beliefs. The stories we tell ourselves about money can hold us back, but with awareness and intentional action, we can rewrite them. I encourage you to start small, incorporating practices like:

- Create a receiving list to celebrate what you've gained each day
- Use affirmations to shift your focus from lack to abundance
- Surround yourself with music or practices that uplift and inspire you.

Remember, the challenges you face, whether financial, emotional or otherwise, don't have to define you. Healing is possible, and it can unlock incredible opportunities for growth and success.

FLOURISHING IN NEW BEGINNINGS

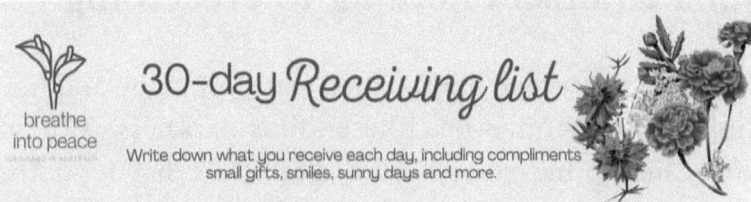

30-day Receiving list

Write down what you receive each day, including compliments, small gifts, smiles, sunny days and more.

DAY 1	DAY 2	DAY 3	DAY 4	DAY 5
DAY 6	DAY 7	DAY 8	DAY 9	DAY 10
DAY 11	DAY 12	DAY 13	DAY 14	DAY 15
DAY 16	DAY 17	DAY 18	DAY 19	DAY 20
DAY 21	DAY 22	DAY 23	DAY 24	DAY 25
DAY 26	DAY 27	DAY 28	DAY 29	DAY 30

©2025 Claire Wu at Breathe Into Peace. All rights reserved.
Only for personal use for the client. Please DO NOT copy or distribute without written consent

Write down what you receive every day. This will help your belief system see all the good things that are coming toward you.

Julia embraces nothing to everything

Julia's story was one of resilience, transformation and finding light in what once felt like endless darkness. When she first came to me, she described her life as 'having nothing'. Financially, emotionally and mentally, she felt depleted. Years of struggling with money had left her paralysed by fear and self-doubt. She had dreams of starting her own business but couldn't imagine how someone like her, someone who felt so unworthy, could make it happen.

Julia's money story ran deep. Growing up, she had absorbed messages about scarcity, unworthiness, and the idea that success was reserved for 'other people'. These beliefs were ingrained into her nervous system, shaping how she approached money and life. Every time she thought about pursuing her business idea, she was overcome with anxiety and a voice in her head whispering, *'Who do you think you are? You have nothing. No-one will buy from you.'*

In our work together, we didn't just talk about business strategy or money. We focused on resetting her nervous system, addressing the deep, somatic roots of her money story. Through specific techniques, Julia began to notice the physiological responses that arose when she thought about money – her chest tightening, posture slumping, heart racing, palms sweating and shortened breaths. These responses weren't just physical; they were the embodiment of years of fear, self-doubt and lack.

We worked on calming her nervous system, using body-based approach and self-massage to help her feel safe in her own body. In combination with the body-based exercises, I guided her to revisit those beliefs she had internalised and helped her reframe them, one by one. We replaced the narrative of 'I have nothing' with 'I have everything I need to start moving forward.' Slowly but surely, Julia began to believe it.

She went from 'Who do you think you are' to 'You are Julia.'

From 'No-one will buy from you' to 'One person will benefit from this.'

The transformation wasn't instant, but it was profound. As Julia's nervous system reset, her mind shifted. She started to see opportunities instead of barriers. One day, she reached out to a close friend to share her vision. To her surprise, her friend was not only supportive but eager to help. This gave her the courage to approach her family, who rallied around her, offering encouragement, connections and even small financial contributions to help her get started.

With this newfound support, Julia applied for funding from a local small business program, something she had never felt confident enough to do before. To her amazement, she was approved. She used the funds to start her product business, creating sustainable and local goods that resonated deeply with her personal values.

The momentum kept building. Julia began selling locally, and as word spread about her unique and high-quality products, she received orders from across the country. Within a few years, her business had grown beyond what she could have imagined, shipping products to customers worldwide. Her story became one of inspiration to others, a testament to what's possible when we confront our deepest fears and reclaim our power.

> Julia's success wasn't just financial; it was personal. She no longer saw herself as someone with nothing but as someone with infinite potential. By addressing her money story at its root (her nervous system) she broke free from the patterns that had held her back. Today, Julia not only runs a thriving global business but also carries a deep sense of self-worth and gratitude for the journey that brought her here.

Jonny stops procrastinating and starts taking action

Jonny was a passionate entrepreneur with a big dream, but like many, he found himself trapped in a cycle of procrastination. He was a former director of an electrical company. He had a brilliant business idea, one he was sure could transform lives and bring financial success, but he could never seem to move past the planning stage. Day after day, he would sit at his desk, staring at his to-do list, feeling overwhelmed and frozen. He kept learning new things, went to new courses and watched many YouTube videos. He'd tell himself, 'I'll start tomorrow' but tomorrow never came.

As months went by, Jonny's savings dwindled. He was almost broke, and the pressure of failing weighed heavily on him. He was filled with guilt and shame, constantly berating himself for his inaction. The more he criticised himself, the harder it became to take the first step. Jonny felt like he was caught in a spiral of self-sabotage, watching his dream slip further away with each passing day.

FLOURISHING IN NEW BEGINNINGS

When Jonny reached out to me, he was at his breaking point. He told me he couldn't understand why he couldn't take action, even though he knew what needed to be done. Together, we explored what was really happening beneath the surface. It became clear that his procrastination wasn't laziness or lack of discipline – it was his nervous system responding to fear of rejections and fear of judgement. The thought of launching his business triggered feelings of inadequacy and fear of failure, leaving his body and mind in a frozen state.

We began working on resetting his nervous system. Through guided techniques, Jonny started to recognise the physical sensations that came with his procrastination – the shallow breathing, the racing thoughts and numbness in the body. Using specific techniques and somatic practices, he learned how to regulate his nervous system and bring himself back to a state of calm and connection.

As his nervous system reset, Jonny began to feel safer in his body. He started to 'feel' in his body and he also began to challenge the stories he told himself. The fear of failure was replaced with thoughts that allowed him to grow and take actions. He started to believe that taking imperfect action was better than staying stuck in fear. With this new perspective, Jonny and I created a business plan that included a marketing and sales plan to move forward, breaking down his launch into small, manageable steps so he would not drop back into the frozen state easily.

The transformation was almost immediate. Within 4–6 weeks, Jonny went from procrastinating to taking consistent action. He finalised his product offerings, built his sales pipelines and launched the business. Each step he took reinforced his confidence and momentum.

When launch day came, Jonny was nervous but excited. He had prepared himself emotionally and physically, using the tools he'd learned to stay grounded and focused. The results were beyond what he had imagined. Within the first few months, Jonny made $50,000 in sales. His business took off, and the overwhelming fear that once paralysed him was replaced with a sense of pride and accomplishment.

> Jonny's story became a powerful reminder of the importance of addressing the root causes of procrastination. By resetting his nervous system and embracing a new belief system, he didn't just save his business – he transformed his life. Today, Jonny continues to grow his business with the same courage and determination that got him started, knowing he has the tools to face any challenge.

'Take the first step in faith. You don't have to see the whole staircase, just take the first step.'
– Martin Luther King Jr.

6 limiting beliefs people commonly have

Limiting beliefs are deeply held convictions that constrain us in some way. By believing them, we end up diminishing ourselves and our ability to achieve our goals.

FLOURISHING IN NEW BEGINNINGS

1. I'm not good enough

This belief undermines self-esteem and can stop individuals from pursuing opportunities because they feel they do not measure up to others or are inherently incapable of achieving success.

2. I don't have enough time

This belief can lead people to procrastinate on pursuing their goals or neglect personal development because they assume they are too busy to change or improve their circumstances.

3. It's too late for me to start

Often, people believe that there's a 'right age' to begin certain activities, learn new skills, or change careers. This belief limits their potential by making them feel that the window of opportunity has permanently closed.

4. I must be perfect

This belief can cause significant anxiety and can prevent individuals from attempting anything new or challenging due to a fear of not doing it perfectly on the first try. This also increases procrastination, overthinking and delays.

5. I don't deserve success

Some people hold a core belief that they are unworthy of success, which can sabotage their efforts to achieve their goals, as they feel undeserving of the results of their hard work.

6. Change is dangerous

This belief fosters a fear of the unknown and leads to resistance to change, even if the current situation is unsatisfactory or harmful, preventing personal growth or improvement in living conditions.

Challenging these limiting beliefs often requires conscious reflection, seeking evidence to the contrary, and sometimes the help of a professional or specialist to adopt more empowering beliefs.

Healing self-practices for moving past limiting beliefs

Think of one of the beliefs you have identified, then answer these questions.

What did you say to others and to yourself? How negative was the language?

_____
_____
_____

Was what you said true?

_____
_____
_____

Can you feel it in your nervous system? Maybe there's resistance in your body (head, chest, upper abdominals, back)? Note the changes in your body when you have this belief.

_____
_____
_____

Where does this limiting belief come from?

_____
_____
_____

What are the feelings that come up? What's your energy like?

_____
_____
_____

What would you do differently if you were no longer living with this belief? Can you put this into action today?

_____
_____
_____

CHAPTER 14

Awaken Your Purpose and Thrive

One thing I believe keeps me moving forward and helps me manifest speaking opportunities, is that I always live in my purpose and vision, which allows me to thrive in life. I truly think having a purpose is so important.

When we begin to wonder about our purpose, the truth is, our purpose is often trying to find us. It might not be something grand, perfect or traditionally 'honourable'. Your purpose is unique to you; it reflects what you've experienced, what you believe and what resonates deeply within you. It can be as simple as wanting a happy family, spreading joy or making the world a better place. Your purpose supports, informs and assists you in achieving your goals, solving problems or exploring new ideas. Whether you're offering services, selling products, sharing knowledge, performing on stage or organising events, your purpose helps you stay anchored during life's challenges.

There are times when I lost my purpose, and my path was muddy and unclear. I got upset and stressed, but I also knew it was going to be a period of transition. I understood that I might need to wait for the answer to come to me, or take the time to figure it out.

My purpose has shifted over time – from helping people to move and be free of chronic pain, to supporting movement and mobility, and now to helping people heal their nervous systems and thrive. This evolution reminds me that our purpose is not static; it's okay if it grows and changes as we do. Each year, our purpose may shift, enriching our lives with colour and diversity, because it's all part of our unique, individual journey.

Big or small, your purpose matters because it's yours.

> *'Your purpose in life is to find your purpose and give your whole heart and soul to it.'*
> *– Buddha*

For some, a life purpose may be nurturing a family, helping others or creating art. For others, it might be innovating solutions to global challenges, spreading joy or simply living with integrity and authenticity. Your life purpose is deeply personal, evolving as you experience life and learn more about yourself.

I love my purpose. It enables me to travel and be in nature while helping people to reset their nervous system and thrive in work and life.

From CEO to someone with schizophrenia

I once worked for an organisation dedicated to advocating for individuals with schizophrenia. This mental health condition is profoundly challenging, affecting not only those diagnosed but also their families and communities. People with schizophrenia often experience severe symptoms, including delusions, hallucinations and distorted perceptions of reality. These symptoms can become chronic, deeply impacting how they think, feel and behave. Schizophrenia creates a disconnect from reality, frequently leading to psychosis and significant disruptions in cognitive and functional abilities. For many, even performing daily tasks can feel insurmountable.

During my time with the organisation, I encountered many stories, but one stands out – a story of a highly successful CEO, Jack, whose life took an abrupt and unexpected turn. Jack had built a thriving career at the helm of a leading company. By all outward appearances, he was the epitome of success: respected in his field, financially secure and admired by colleagues. But one day, everything changed.

Jack experienced a severe psychotic episode that marked the onset of schizophrenia. It was as if his world had been turned upside down overnight. His diagnosis shattered the life he had meticulously built. The ripple effects were devastating: his partner left him, his children distanced themselves, and he found himself institutionalised, grappling with a condition he had never imagined confronting.

Schizophrenia had stripped away not just his career but also the relationships and stability he had taken for granted. For a long time, he struggled to make sense of what had happened. The road to recovery was neither quick nor straightforward, but he persisted, gradually piecing his life back together. Eventually, Jack did recover, at least to a point where he could find meaning and purpose in his new reality. He began to rebuild his life, but this time with different priorities. Reflecting on his journey, he shared with me, 'I would never have imagined the things that happened to me. Now, I just want to live each day fully, cherish the time I have, and focus on the present instead of worrying about what might happen 10 or 20 years from now.'

His words carried profound wisdom. They served as a reminder that life is unpredictable. Even at the height of success, unforeseen events can disrupt everything. The question he posed was one that resonated deeply: 'When everything is stripped away, do you have regrets or resentment?'

Jack admitted that the life he once lived, despite its outward success, was not one he truly wanted. He had spent so much time focused on building his career that he had neglected what mattered most: his relationships, his passions, and his own health and wellbeing. He wished he had spent more time with his family and pursued what genuinely fulfilled him.

> Jack's story challenges us to reflect on our own lives. If everything were taken away today, would you have regrets? Are you pursuing what truly matters? Jack's journey is a powerful testament to the resilience of the human spirit and the importance of aligning our lives with our values. It reminds us to cherish the present, nurture our relationships and prioritise what brings us lasting fulfillment.

General manager and advocate for schizophrenia

In my work, I had the privilege of supporting a remarkable individual – a high-functioning general manager, Lina living with schizophrenia. Despite the complexities of her condition, she collaborated actively with government sectors and non-profit organisations, demonstrating an extraordinary commitment to her work and advocacy. Her resilience and dedication, however, were only part of her incredible story.

When we first met, she shared her journey, marked by profound challenges. She had survived sexual trauma, domestic violence and severe abuse, experiences that could have broken even the strongest among us. Instead of succumbing to despair, she channelled her pain into purpose. Driven by a deep desire to raise awareness about domestic violence and sexual abuse, she began speaking publicly about her experiences. Her powerful voice resonated with many, offering hope and shedding light on issues that are often silenced.

Though she was clear about her mission, her past trauma continued to cast a shadow over her life. It manifested as emotional weight, lingering fear and self−doubt. Despite her outward success, she often felt trapped by the memories of her painful experiences. She recognised the need for deeper healing to fully step into her potential.

We embarked on a transformative journey together using trauma−informed techniques to release the pain that's heavily stored in her amygdala. This evidence−based approach helped her process and release the energy and 'alarm' that was inside her body. Through our sessions, she began to feel a profound sense of relief, as if freeing herself from a heavy load she had carried for years.

Healing wasn't just about addressing the past. It was also about creating balance. She realised that her demanding workload was taking a toll on her mental wellness. Together, we worked to restructure her life, focusing on what truly mattered. She cut back on non−essential commitments and redirected her energy toward speaking engagements that aligned with her mission. This shift allowed her to focus on what she loved most: inspiring others and making a difference. Self-care became a cornerstone of her transformation. For someone who had spent years putting others first, learning to care for herself was both challenging and rewarding. Simple acts of self-compassion, like setting boundaries, taking time to rest and prioritising her wellbeing, helped her build a stronger foundation.

Her journey is a testament to the power of purpose and healing. By addressing her trauma and realigning her life with her values, she discovered a renewed sense of freedom and strength. Her story reminds us that even the most painful experiences can be transformed into sources of meaning and growth when paired with a clear purpose and the courage to heal.

> Lisa's experience reaffirmed for me the profound resilience of the human spirit. It showed that purpose is not just a guide through life's challenges but a catalyst for turning even the darkest moments into opportunities for connection, advocacy and hope.

An engineer overcame his PTSD

Nikola was a high-achieving Fortune-100 engineer earning a substantial salary and living what many would consider a dream life. With a steady career, supportive family and a comfortable lifestyle, he seemed to have everything anyone could want. But behind the polished exterior, Nikola was battling something he rarely shared: post-traumatic stress disorder (PTSD).

The symptoms were relentless. Sleepless nights, vivid flashbacks and a constant state of anxiety left him feeling restless and disconnected. Despite seeing psychiatrists and psychologists and trying various therapies, Nikola still felt trapped in his own body.

'I've done everything they recommended,' he confided during our first session. 'Counselling and medication have helped, but I still feel this deep, unshakable tension in my body. It's like I can't breathe fully or relax. I feel the pain in my body.'

Together, we decided to focus on a holistic approach to healing, starting with the body. Nikola began a tailored program designed to reset his nervous system. The goal was not just to calm his mind but to release the trauma stored in his body. Through a combination of deep breathing, with specific patterns of intense inhale and exhale, he started to notice subtle shifts.

At first, it was just moments of clarity, where he felt present for a few seconds longer than usual. Then it grew into something more. Over the weeks, Nikola reported better sleep, fewer flashbacks, and an overall sense of calm that had been missing for years. After 8–10 weeks, he no longer qualified for the symptoms of PTSD. As we repaired his nervous system, his confidence and creativity slowly returned. 'For the first time in ages, I feel like I can think clearly,' he told me.

That clarity led him to reconnect with a passion he'd buried long ago – creating unique ice cream flavours. As a child,

Nikola had loved experimenting in the kitchen, blending exotic spices and ingredients to create desserts that delighted his family and friends. With his newfound energy and focus, Nikola decided to turn this passion into a project. He started small, making batches of ice cream for friends and neighbours. The response was overwhelming. People loved the bold, unexpected flavours he crafted, like saffron–cardamum and rose–pistachio. Encouraged by the enthusiasm, he launched a local ice cream brand, focusing on artisan flavours inspired by his cultural roots.

The project quickly gained traction. Nikola's ice cream became the talk of his community, then expanded to cafes and specialty stores. Within 6 months, he had turned his passion into a thriving business. On Mother's Day (a particularly busy sales day) he sold out within hours, a moment he described as both surreal and deeply fulfilling. Today, Nikola continues to grow his business while inspiring others with his story. 'Healing isn't just about letting go of pain,' he says. 'It's about creating space for joy and purpose. And for me, that purpose is my inner child's dream.'

> Reflecting on his journey, Nikola realised that overcoming PTSD wasn't just about managing symptoms – it was about rediscovering himself. Through resetting the nervous system, he not only found relief from the physical and emotional weight of his trauma but also unlocked a part of himself that had been buried for years.

> *'Purpose is the place where your deep
> gladness meets the world's needs.'*
> – Frederick Buechner

Why do we have a purpose?

Our life purpose is the reason we feel we exist, the unique combination of values, passions and talents that guide how we contribute to the world and find fulfillment. It's not necessarily tied to a career or achievement; it's about what gives our life meaning and motivates us to grow, connect and thrive.

Having a purpose fulfills a fundamental human need for meaning. It provides a sense of direction, helping you prioritise what matters most. It anchors you during challenging times, acting as a guiding light to keep you focused and steady. When you're aligned with your purpose, you feel energised and passionate about life. It drives motivation, propelling you to take meaningful action and face obstacles with determination.

Studies show that having a purpose contributes to both mental and physical health. It can reduce stress, boost happiness and even improve longevity, enhancing overall wellbeing.

Purpose often involves making a positive impact on others or the world. This connection fosters deeper relationships and creates a sense of belonging to a larger community. It also challenges you to grow, adapt and evolve. By reminding you of the bigger picture, purpose helps you overcome setbacks and build resilience.

Living in alignment with your purpose brings a profound sense of satisfaction. It makes your efforts feel worthwhile, filling your life with fulfillment and joy.

How do we discover our purpose?

Purpose isn't always something we find – it often finds us. It reveals itself through our experiences, values and the things that deeply resonate with us. Making time for self-reflection can help uncover it.

It's important to remember that our purpose can evolve. What feels meaningful in one phase of life may shift as we grow and change. And that's okay – it's part of the journey.

Ultimately, our life purpose is about finding what fulfills us and sharing that fulfillment with the world. It's not about perfection or grandiosity but about living authentically and making the most of the unique gifts and experiences we bring to life.

Healing self-practices for uncovering your purpose

What are the things that make me lose track of time?
_____
_____
_____

What impact do I want to have on others?
_____
_____
_____

What brings me joy or a sense of accomplishment?
_____
_____
_____

What do I want to be remembered for?
_____
_____
_____

What did I wish I could become when I was a child?
_____
_____
_____

CHAPTER 15

You Are Not Broken, You Are Simply Human

It took me over 10 years to get to this point. From moving to Europe, then from Finland to Singapore, and from Singapore to Australia, the journey spanned over a decade. During this time, my nervous system and belief system shifted significantly, from 'I hate you so much and I hate everything around me' to 'I love people around me, I love myself, and I love all the things happening in my life'. Yes, it takes a lot of courage and consistent practice. There are moments when you might fall back or relapse, but that's okay. It's part of the process, part of being human. What matters is continuing to move forward, one step at a time.

I still vividly remember waking up one morning and suddenly feeling amazing. Tears of joy streamed down my cheeks as I reflected on everything I'd been through, from being suicidal, enduring domestic violence, toxic relationships and unhealthy workplaces, to arriving at this moment. I appreciated all the experiences that shaped me, and I marvelled at the strength and resilience that brought me to where I am today. Looking back, even though there were times I regretted my choices, I now see how they contributed to my growth.

I majored in physiotherapy with a minor in psychology. My parents didn't allow me to take psychology as a major because they thought it was 'for crazy people'. Instead, I studied physiotherapy and pursued psychology on the side, eventually completing a master's degree in biomechanics in Europe. While the studies were challenging, and I didn't enjoy the hands–on aspects like massaging clients or adjusting spines through mobilisations or manipulations, I found joy in teaching body–based exercise. The anatomy, physiology and biology I learned in school have taken my career to heights I never imagined.

Although I didn't become a psychologist or run my own clinics, I ventured out to build my own courses and programs. Teaching what I practice every day has allowed me to integrate my life experiences and the knowledge I've gained from working with clients. I feel honoured to contribute to the health and wellness space, particularly with high achievers facing obstacles. My expertise in anatomy, psychology, neuroscience, the nervous system and personal development has guided me down the path of entrepreneurship. Along the way, I've also embraced skills like marketing and sales, which have shaped me into the person I am today.

YOU ARE NOT BROKEN, YOU ARE SIMPLY HUMAN

Sometimes, people think I'm crazy for investing tens of thousands of dollars in personal development. But if I hadn't made those investments, I wouldn't be where I am now, and I wouldn't be as happy, content or successful as I am now. I encourage you to appreciate the knowledge you already have rather than focusing on what you lack. Growth is ongoing, and every small breakthrough deserves celebration. Whether it's opening a bottle of champagne, visiting a favourite restaurant, or taking few hours off, celebrating progress reinforces our motivation and resilience.

I've also learned to embrace my imperfections, like being 10 minutes late or overbooking my schedule. By creating buffers between meetings and allowing white space in my work, I've found flexibility and balance. Each state of being serves a purpose, and honouring the need to rest helps me fully accept myself, flaws and all. Reframing weaknesses as strengths has been transformative.

Self-compassion is like a muscle; the more you practise, the stronger it becomes. When you make mistakes, replace harsh self-criticism with neutral or kind thoughts. Embrace yourself fully, imperfections and all. Detach your self-worth from external metrics like income. Success isn't about hitting a specific number; it's about loving what you do and being at peace with who you are. Celebrate progress, prioritise self-care, and schedule joyful activities regularly. This will not only enrich your life but also train your brain to appreciate the present moment and build lasting confidence. I came from a family that valued perfectionism, and I often got in my own way. I self-sabotaged or I tried to achieve perfection so I could avoid shame and pain. As I say, our nervous system needs flexibility. We need to move between fight or flight and freeze state and come back to flow state, where we rest and connect with others. Each state serves a purpose, and honouring my need for rest helps me fully accept myself and embrace my flaws. (You can get get into flow 3x audio here: https://breatheintopeace.com/products/fa)

Many of you might feel shame or guilt for not being perfect. You might hate your weaknesses, your downsides, or specific parts of yourself that you don't like. But the truth is, those parts of you contribute to your uniqueness. For example, being 5 minutes late or having a fully booked schedule is a part of me. While I'm learning to create more balance and be on time, I've also reframed these traits into something positive. Rather than trying to eliminate weaknesses, I focus on seeing them differently. You can reframe weaknesses into strengths or develop other strengths that overshadow them.

It's okay to make mistakes. I've made plenty in my business and life. For instance, at a festival, I made many sales and connections but forgot to collect people's emails. I missed out on hundreds of potential contacts. But I've learned to be self–compassionate. I reminded myself that it was my first time at the festival, and it's okay to make mistakes. Next time, I'll remember. Practising self–compassion when you make mistakes is critical, and it's a skill that improves with practice, much like gratitude. To be more self–compassionate, start by being kind to yourself. If you catch yourself thinking, 'I always mess things up' or 'I'm terrible at this' try shifting those thoughts to something more neutral like, 'I made a mistake' or 'I didn't do this well, but I can learn and grow'. Practising kind self–talk is essential.

Embrace yourself fully, imperfections and all. Don't let setbacks or mistakes define your worth. For example, I don't let the monthly income from my business dictate my self-worth. Whether I make $5,000 this month or $10,000 one month or $20,000 the next, it doesn't change my value as a person. Detaching your self-worth from external measures like money or achievements is crucial for thriving in business and life.

Many of my clients struggle with perfectionism and tying their success to arbitrary milestones. I worked with one client who believed he wasn't successful because he hadn't made a million dollars yet, despite running a thriving digital marketing business. This belief led to burnout and hindered his progress. We worked on detaching his self-worth from financial goals, celebrating his achievements, and embracing self-love. As he focused on doing what he loved and serving his clients, his business flourished.

Finally, prioritise self-care. Balance your work with activities that nourish and bring you joy. Schedule time with family, friends or simply for yourself. Engaging in pleasurable activities trains your brain to enjoy the present moment and fosters confidence and self-love. Remember to appreciate yourself, celebrate your progress and embrace who you are, imperfections and all. If you seek help, you will get help and you will be helped. Find help for what you need during challenging times. That's exactly what I did when I was 18 years old, and look at where it led me. I learned to reset my nervous system and rewire my belief system.

The girl that stood at the edge of the rooftop, if she had jumped, would not be travelling the world, meeting new people, getting her therapy licenses from three different countries, experiencing exotic cultures and foods, having fun times, working with clients, running her own business ... If she didn't heal from the pain and sh*t her family left her, she would be crying, ruminating, carrying all the baggage in her life. She would not be able to enjoy, to love, to laugh, to chant, to dance, to lift weights, to hike in forests, to swim in the ocean and to live again happily and fully.

When I was first diagnosed with anxiety and depression, and my psychologist told me that I had trauma, it really hurt to hear the word 'trauma'. I thought I was broken, that I wasn't enough or worthy. I didn't like the word 'trauma' because it felt like there was something wrong or defective about me. Eventually, I clarified this with my therapist and practitioners. I learned that trauma isn't unique to me, it's something that happens to a lot of people. In fact, I believe we all have our share of challenges in life. As humans, we go through ups and downs, and studies show that close to 80% of people experience trauma at some point.

Trauma is an event that involves exposure to actual or threatened death, serious injury, sexual violence or other potentially overwhelming events. It can be physical or mental, and everyone responds differently. Trauma becomes traumatic when something happens too fast, too soon, or too much for our bodies and emotions to process, so it gets stored in the amygdala. When we're triggered, the alarm goes off in our amygdala, and we feel it in our body – for example, sweaty palms, shortness of breaths, fast heartbeat and dilated pupils.

Some people recover with the support of friends and family, while others need professional help. In Australia, common traumatic events include unexpected deaths of loved ones, witnessing someone being killed or injured, or life–threatening car accidents. However, trauma can also result from multiple small events that add up over time. Many survivors face long-term physical, emotional, cognitive and even financial consequences that can affect their lives, families and communities for years.

Trauma is also linked to mental issues like anxiety, depression, substance abuse, self-harm and even suicide. Childhood trauma, in particular, increases the risk of developing mental illness and can also affect how we respond to treatment. The reality is that most of us have been through different challenges, some larger, some smaller, but comparing our experiences isn't helpful. Trauma isn't about whose experience is 'better' or 'worse', it's about acknowledging that no-one's pain is invalid.

Being human means accepting that there's no such thing as perfection. Most of us are doing the best we can, and we should extend grace and kindness to ourselves and others. To be human is to live in our bodies and recognise that we're spiritual beings having a human experience – feeling it, living it and being in it. Our humanity is shaped by our consciousness, empathy, creativity, resilience and our pursuit of meaning and purpose. These are the tools that help us navigate the challenges of life.

My methodology and signature program – Reset & Thrive focus on the emotional pain and physical pain stored in the body, self worth, relationships and integration. From the body-up, we work on feeling safe in the body through customised solutions for your unique nervous system. From the brain-down, we work on rewiring beliefs and neural pathways to improve your overall nervous system health over time.

It's okay to feel triggered sometimes. Acknowledging the trigger is the first step, and it helps to understand that being easily triggered might stem from past experiences or external stress. Unresolved trauma and negative experiences can make us more sensitive to stressors. High stress levels and external challenges can make us more reactive rather than responsive.

But here's the thing: life includes a lot of sh*t and hardship. You might face challenges again, and that's okay. Our goal isn't to eliminate all the sh*t in life, it's to find ways to live with and manage it. There's no point in trying to avoid every bad event because life is unpredictable. What matters is finding ways to handle stress, master your nervous system, and navigate tough times with resilience.

When sh*t happens, it's natural to feel upset, to blame others or ourselves. But focusing on how we respond rather than what's out of our control can help us turn things around. Acknowledge what you've been through, celebrate the fact that you've made it this far, and recognise your strength and growth. If you're reading this, you're alive, breathing and improving yourself – and that's worth cheering and celebrating.

> *'Everybody faces pain. Everybody has sh*t in life.'*
> *– Hunter Biden*

> Remember, it's not about perfection; it's about progress. By embracing a new perspective and finding practical ways to address adversity, you can move forward with greater confidence. You may not be able to control everything, but you can control how you treat yourself during difficult times. Self-compassion, hope and a belief in the ups and downs of life can make all the difference. Bad things may come in threes, but good things often come in sixes. Life is full of contrasts, and that's what makes it uniquely ours.

Lisa's overcame criticism

Lisa, a vibrant and hardworking professional in her mid-30s, came to me feeling overwhelmed by how certain situations would completely derail her day. She had been dealing with triggers tied to past experiences of loss, rejection and self-doubt. Lisa described these triggers as emotional landmines, unexpected and intense reactions that would pull her back into a spiral of anxiety and sadness.

When we first began working together, Lisa was unsure why seemingly small things, like a critical comment from a colleague or a song from her childhood, could evoke such strong emotions. Her body would tense, her thoughts would race, and she'd feel the overwhelming need to escape. Lisa often avoided situations where she feared these reactions might arise, which affected her relationships, career and overall happiness.

Through our sessions, we identified her primary triggers and worked to understand the stories and beliefs tied to them. One major trigger was criticism, rooted in her childhood experiences with a highly critical parent. Every time Lisa felt criticised, it activated the fear of 'not being good enough', causing her to shut down emotionally or lash out defensively.

The first step in Lisa's healing journey was awareness. We explored how her body and mind reacted to triggers, giving her the tools to recognise when she was being triggered in real time. I taught Lisa grounding techniques like deep breathing, naming five things she could see around her and consciously relaxing her shoulders and jaw. These simple tools helped her stay present instead of being swept away by emotional waves.

Next, we focused on reframing her triggers. Lisa learned that her reactions weren't a sign of weakness but rather her body's way of signalling unresolved pain. Together, we unpacked these emotions and reframed them as opportunities for growth. For instance, instead of viewing criticism as a personal failure, Lisa began to see it as feedback that she could assess and choose how to act on.

An essential part of her journey was releasing stored pain from her body. We worked with somatic techniques that allowed Lisa to process emotions she had long suppressed, particularly in the fascia and muscles. Simple practices, like gentle spinal movement, helped her connect with and release the tension stored in her nervous system. Over time, Lisa noticed that situations that once felt unbearable now felt manageable.

We also explored her inner dialogue. Lisa replaced harsh self-criticism with kind, affirming statements. Instead of thinking,

'I can't believe I let this upset me again', she learned to say, 'It's okay to feel this way. I am learning and growing.' This shift in her inner voice was transformative, allowing her to approach her triggers with curiosity and kindness rather than judgement.

Finally, Lisa practised building resilience. She challenged herself to face situations she once avoided, like speaking up in meetings or having honest conversations with loved ones. Each small victory reinforced her confidence and proved to her that she was stronger than her fears.

> After several months, Lisa reflected on her progress with pride. She no longer saw herself as a victim of her triggers but as someone empowered to navigate them. While they didn't disappear entirely, Lisa gained the tools to manage them and live a fuller, more balanced life. Her journey serves as a testament to the power of self-awareness, self-compassion and consistent effort in overcoming life's challenges. Instead of her nervous system taking control, she took control over of her nervous system.

Angela recovered from triggers

Angela, a compassionate and talented woman in her early 40s, reached out to me during a particularly difficult season in her life. She was struggling with triggers that often left her feeling overwhelmed, paralysed and unsure of how to move forward. Angela described her triggers as deeply rooted in past experiences, especially from her childhood and early adult years, when she faced neglect, rejection and self-doubt.

Her triggers manifested in various ways. A simple disagreement with her partner could spiral into a feeling of abandonment. The sound of raised voices reminded her of conflict-ridden moments from her childhood, leaving her heart racing and her body tense. At work, constructive feedback felt like personal criticism, causing her to shut down emotionally or overwork to prove her worth.

Angela's first breakthrough came from understanding that triggers are the body's way of signalling unresolved pain or trauma. We worked together to identify her most common triggers and the patterns of reaction tied to them. She began to notice the early signs – a clenched jaw, a racing mind or the urge to withdraw from her body. This self-awareness was a pivotal step, allowing Angela to recognise when she was being triggered in real time.

To help Angela regain a sense of control, we introduced somatic techniques. She practised them to calm her nervous system, focusing on the rhythm of her breath until her racing thoughts subsided. Angela also used visualisation techniques, imagining herself in a safe and peaceful place when her emotions felt overwhelming. These tools allowed her to stay present and avoid being swept up by the tidal wave of her triggers.

As we explored the roots of her triggers, Angela realised that many stemmed from her past and childhood, beliefs like, 'I'm not good enough' or 'I don't deserve love unless I'm perfect.' Together, we worked on reframing these narratives. Angela began to challenge the validity of these beliefs and replace them with empowering ones, like, 'I am enough just as I am' and 'I deserve love and acceptance.'

Angela also incorporated somatic practices to help her release stored tension in her body. Simple movements, like shaking out her arms or practising gentle spinal movement, helped her let go of the physical stress that accompanied her emotional reactions. Journalling became another powerful tool for Angela, allowing her to process her emotions and reflect on her growth. A key aspect of Angela's healing was cultivating self–compassion. Instead of beating herself up for being 'too sensitive' or 'not strong enough', she learned to speak to herself with kindness. She began to see her triggers not as a sign of weakness but as a natural part of her healing journey.

Over time, Angela noticed a significant shift. Situations that once overwhelmed her no longer had the same grip on her. She learned to respond rather than react. For example, instead of shutting down after a disagreement, she would pause, practise somatic techniques, and express her feelings calmly. At work, she started embracing feedback as an opportunity for growth rather than a threat to her self–worth.

> Angela's journey wasn't without setbacks, but each step forward reinforced her confidence. She transformed her relationship with her triggers, seeing them as opportunities to practise resilience and self–love. Angela now approaches life with a newfound sense of balance and empowerment, showcasing the strength within her to heal and thrive.

> '*Wounds won't heal the way you want them to.*
> *They heal the way they need to.*'
> *– Dele Olanubi*

What are triggers?

Triggers are stimuli that cause an emotional, physical or psychological reaction, often tied to past experiences or trauma. Triggers can remind someone of a distressing event, causing them to react in ways that might feel overwhelming, uncontrollable or disproportionate to the current situation. These reactions often stem from how the brain and body process and store memories of difficult experiences. Common triggers include:

- Emotional triggers: Specific words, phrases or actions that evoke intense emotions, such as fear, anger, sadness or guilt
- Sensory triggers: Sights, sounds, smells, tastes or physical sensations that remind someone of a past experience (e.g. the smell of smoke reminding someone of a fire)
- Situational triggers: Environments, settings or social interactions that replicate aspects of a traumatic event (e.g. crowded spaces for someone with trauma related to an accident)
- Cognitive triggers: Certain thoughts, memories or reminders of the past that bring up feelings of distress.

Triggers activate the brain's amygdala, which is responsible for processing emotions like fear and stress. When the amygdala perceives a threat (even if it's not an actual danger in the present), it can cause the body to go into a 'fight, flight or freeze' response. This reaction is the body's way of protecting itself, even if the danger is no longer present.

The common reactions to triggers can be divided to four categories: emotional (intense feelings of fear, sadness, anger or shame), physical (sweating, rapid heartbeat, tightness in the chest or nausea), behavioural (avoidance of certain situations, lashing out or becoming withdrawn) and mental (flashbacks, intrusive thoughts or difficulty focusing).

How can we deal with triggers?

- Awareness: recognising what triggers you and understanding the connection to past experiences.

- Grounding techniques: strategies like deep breathing, focusing on your surroundings, or practising mindfulness to stay present.

- Self–compassion: being kind to yourself when triggered and acknowledging that your response is valid.

- Professional help: therapy or counselling to process and work through trauma and build coping strategies.

- Building resilience: Strengthening your nervous system through practices like tapping, breathwork or somatic techniques.

Triggers are a normal part of life, especially for those who have experienced trauma. Learning to recognise and manage them can help you respond more effectively and reduce their impact on your wellbeing.

You don't need to be fixed

The work I do is not a quick fix. In fact, you don't need fixing because you're not broken, torn or falling apart. Everything that has happened to you, all the difficult, painful moments, is a part of you.

Have you heard of the concept of Kintsugi? Kintsugi is the Japanese art of repairing broken ceramics with lacquer mixed with gold, silver or platinum. The idea is to embrace imperfections and recognise the beauty in flaws. When you look at a piece repaired with Kintsugi, the cracks filled with gold make it even more stunning than the original, whole ceramic. It's a reminder that when things fall apart, you can put them back together and create something beautiful from the brokenness. This philosophy holds a powerful lesson for us as humans. When life shatters, we can use the pieces to build strength and beauty. It's not about erasing the past but about transforming it.

I want you to practise forgiveness as a way of letting go. Start by writing down the things you want to forgive – situations, people or even yourself. List 10 to 20 items. It could be forgiving yourself for mistakes, forgiving someone who hurt you, or releasing anger toward a situation. Once you've written the list, go through each item and say: 'Yes, thank you. I love you. I forgive you.' Forgiveness isn't just about others; it's about clearing mental space and reclaiming peace.

When we hold on to negativity, it clutters our mind and blocks us from exploring opportunities. Letting go creates room to grow. After going through your list, imagine putting the emotional baggage down, stepping over it, and using it as a stepping stone to move forward.

Another tool that can support your healing is having a routine. While it may sound simple or cliché, a structured routine reduces anxiety and creates stability. When we have predictable habits, it helps calm our mind, improves productivity and builds better time management. For instance, my evening routine includes a gym session at 6 pm, followed by dinner and relaxation routines with tapping, meditations and rocking. My mornings start with journalling to process thoughts, breathwork to energise or ground myself, and a short meditation tailored to the day's intention. These routines keep me aligned, productive and balanced.

If you don't have a routine, start small, perhaps with a consistent wake-up time or a simple morning ritual. Focus on three key priorities daily to avoid overwhelm, and include at least one activity you genuinely enjoy. Be consistent but flexible, adapting as needed. Celebrate small wins, track your progress through journalling, and remind yourself that you're doing your best.

Getting over life's challenges doesn't happen overnight. It's a gradual process. The pain and patterns we carry often took years to develop, but with consistent practice, healing is possible. Start with small, intentional steps, and over time, you'll create a life of peace, joy and purpose.

Remember, getting over your sh*t is just the start. The real goal is to live fully and enjoy the life you've built.

Healing self-practices for managing triggers

What are my triggers?

1. _____
2. _____
3. _____

How intense is my trigger? 1 being minimal and 10 being very uncomfortable
_____

Where do I feel it in my body when I am triggered?
_____

What do I currently do when I'm triggered? Is it a good coping mechanism?
_____
_____
_____

What nervous system state am I in when I am triggered?
_____

What else can I do when I'm triggered?
_____
_____
_____

FINAL WORDS

This is Only the Start of Your New Beginning

I hope that the stories, frameworks and tools I've shared with you in this book helped you let go of the sh*t that's holding you back so you can move forward in your life. As you close this book, pause for a moment to reflect on how far you've come. You've chosen to face your challenges head—on, to unpack the layers of sh*t that weighed you down and to rewrite your narrative. That is no small feat. It's courageous, messy and powerful.

When we learn about the practical tools available to shift our belief system and our nervous system, we can understand our triggers, nervous system state and the stories behind the reasons we take certain actions. When we gain control over our nervous system, we take control of our lives – our relationships, work, leisure, community and finance.

The things that happened to us, those that are outside our control, like our parents, our society, our schools and our peers, can feel like a burden, painful and hurting. We might feel like we cannot get through it and feel held back. But that's not the reality.

Suppose we can start to take charge, observe, find tools to regulate, shift the belief system, and understand the triggers. In that case, we can navigate challenges easily and confidently, because we can handle the situations and manage our nervous system to return to ourselves.

Your belief system and your nervous system are unique. It's like your fingerprint. The more you understand them, the better you are able to move between each state in your nervous system. The more self-awareness you have around your feelings, triggers and tools, the better you are at getting through them.

Getting over your sh*t doesn't mean eliminating every bad day, negative thought or painful memory. Life doesn't work that way. Instead, it's about reclaiming your power and learning how to navigate those moments with grace and resilience. It's about choosing growth over stagnation, self-compassion over self-criticism, and authenticity over the mask you thought you had to wear.

Throughout these pages, you've been handed tools – practical strategies, shifts and actionable exercises. But like any tools, they

THIS IS ONLY THE START OF YOUR NEW BEGINNING

only work if you use them consistently. The transformation you're seeking isn't a one-time event; it's a daily practice. Each time you choose to challenge a limiting belief, overcome a trigger, return from a fight or flight state, return from shut down, connect with others, set a boundary or nurture your wellbeing, you're reinforcing the new, empowered version of yourself.

Your journey deserves to be celebrated, every step of the way. Sometimes the wins are big, like finally leaving a toxic relationship or launching a dream project. Other times, they could be getting out of bed on a hard day, saying 'no' without guilt, or catching yourself before spiralling into self-sabotage or self-doubt. Each victory matters, because it proves to you that change is happening.

Growth isn't linear, setbacks happen and sometimes we can go back or go around our struggles over and over again. But they don't erase progress. When those moments arise, meet yourself with kindness instead of judgement, meet yourself with compassion instead of criticism. Remind yourself that you're still learning and evolving.

As you transform, you'll notice something extraordinary: you will see the growth ripples out to those around you. When you show up authentically, others feel inspired to do the same. When you set healthy boundaries, you model self-respect. And when you choose joy, you invite others to join you in that space. Your journey isn't just about you, it's about the impact you make simply by being your best self.

So here we are, at the end of this book but the beginning of a new chapter in your life. What will you do with the wisdom, tools and strength you've gained? Will you take the leap you've been postponing? Will you reconnect with the passion you buried? Will you finally give yourself permission to live fully and unapologetically?

Whatever you choose, remember this: you're not starting from scratch. You're starting from experience, with a foundation built on resilience, courage and self−awareness. You've got what it takes to create a life that feels true to you.

Now, go out there and show the world what happens when you decide to get over your sh★t and thrive.

With love and belief in you,

Claire Elvera Wu

Building Breathe Into Peace was fun, I got the chance to speak at multiple festivals, trade shows, events, business groups and even collaborate with award-winning First Nations Artists.

PS: You can always start with the initial personalised plans for your nervous system, belief system and understand your current state. You can book an initial 90−min assessment here to get a baseline

THIS IS ONLY THE START OF YOUR NEW BEGINNING

and learn about various states, triggers and current plans: https://breatheintopeace.com/products/90–min–initial–assessment?

I also have other offers as well. Please find the table below and feel free to book a call to chat further.

RESET: Pathway to Profits Masterclass 90-Min Live	Reset&Thrive 90-Day Mastermind	Aligned Business Success Inner Circle 6-Month
Break free from Overwhelm	Initial & Post Nervous System Assessment (Emotional/Physical)	Initial & Post Business Assessment
VIP Upgrade: ☑ Live 90-minute Masterclass ☑ Guided Reset ☑ 10-Day Sales Action Plan ☑ Access to Replay Recording	Free eBook for all attendees- 30-day self-care ebook ☑ Vault of techniques ☑ VIP Retreat Day ☑ Workshops ☑ Access to Replay Recording	Free eBook for all attendees- 30-day business ebook ☑ Vault of techniques ☑ VIP Retreat Day ☑ Workshops ☑ Access to Replay Recording
5-Day Reset Application	90-Min Fortnightly Live Group Coaching	90-Min Fortnightly Live Group Coaching
	90-Min Private Coaching	90-Min Private coaching
	Group Messenger Support	Group Messenger Support
	Resources Link to all attendees, including the eBook, vault of techniques, mental wellness checklist	Resources: Link to all attendees, including eBook, business energetics, business wellness checklist

Keynotes & Workshops Available

Breathe Into Peace Pty Ltd helps you achieve high performance, build mental resilience without burnout. We specialise in resetting the nervous system to help you thrive in work and life. There are 45-minute keynote and 3-hour workshops, 90-day and 10-month programs and speaking available for companies, associations, hospitals and schools looking to improve mental wellness with practical tools for everyday use.

Inquire to admin@breatheintopeace.com

Claire Wu

Motivational & Resilience Speaker
Resilience & Nervous System
Specialist for High Performance

About

Claire helps organizations and individuals turn stress into strategy, starting with the nervous system. As director of RESET & THRIVE™, she equips high-performing teams with science-backed tools to reduce burnout, boost focus, and increase emotional regulation. Her sessions deliver measurable improvements in energy, engagement, and leadership.

With 15+ years in health and wellness, Claire has spoken at major conferences and been recognized as a Business xCellence and Women Changing the World finalist. More than accolades, it's her ability to shift culture and performance that sets her apart. When your people reset, your business thrives.

Keynote Topics

Empowering Leaders with Resilience

- Increase confidence and success
- Build stronger professional & personal relationships

Master Your Stress for High Performance

- High productivity and performance
- Increase clarify, focus, and resilience.

Breaking Burnout Cycle

- Restore energy and drive
- Create sustainable high performance

Testimonials

I highly recommend anyone to Claire's workshop I learned techniques that I will do every day!
- Praveen, OCBC Op Manager

I love it and I really enjoy the talk! Claire blends humour, knowledge and simple tools for mental health. I recommend anyone who has a stressful and busy life. -Giselle, Tech Sales Manager

Claire is a very engaging workshop facilitator and she gives our team to interact and ask questions. She generously shared with us her journey in mental wellness and resilience
- Jenny , Estia Health,Executive Director

Contact Me

 claire@breatheintopeace.com
 www.breatheintopeace/keynote-speaking
 +61-408-082-032

As Seen On

www.ingramcontent.com/pod-product-compliance
Lightning Source LLC
Chambersburg PA
CBHW030318080526
44584CB00012B/605